Copyrigh

MW00916207

The characters and events portrayed in this book are fictitious. Any similarity to real persons, living or dead, is coincidental and not intended by the author.

ISBN-13: 9798798395644
ISBN-10: 1477123456

Cover design by: Art Painter
Library of Congress Control Number: 2018675309
Printed in the United States of America

CONTENTS

Peace of Mind

The Prince of Peace
Keeps Believers in
Perfect Peace

Yvonne Tiburzi Knotts

Contributors :
Typist: Mary Jane Whitaker
Editor: Adam Grigsby
Photographer: Lacey McComas

This book is dedicated to my Mom and God who both inspired me, encouraged me, and gave me love and support to complete this book.

I want to give a special thankful appreciation for the Holy Spirit speaking to the following people who helped me achieve writing the book Peace of mind.

Pastor Suzi Hancock Nowak propelled me to write my first Christian book when she said 'some of you have a gift to write that book".

Pastor Medina Pullings encouraged me when she said 'finish writing that book" "finish what you started".

Pastor Kim Jones encouraged me when she said "do not worry about grammar or punctuation, as you write your book".

Pastor Karen Carpenter lead me to message her if any one needed help to get a book published so I had to hirer a typist and editor.

Mary Jane Whitaker was so patient being my typist as I rewrote paragraphs over and over.

Pastor Mary Nowak Fraker spoke in the Heavenly language and interpreted in English and said "keep writing, it over and over" so the Holy Spirit lead me to rewrite all five chapters over.

Adam Grigsby did a professional job editing all five chapters.

Works referenced in this book:

The Complete Guide to Your Emotions & Health by Emrika Padus

Taking Out Your Emotional Trash by Georgia Shaffer

Lord, Change My Attitude by James MacDonald

Battlefield of the Mind by Joyce Meyer

Counseling Through Your Bible Handbook by June Hunt

Deadly Emotions by Don Colbert, M.D.

Getting Anger Under Control by Neil T. Anderson & Rich Miller

How to have Freedom from Fear Worry and Your Case of Nerves by A.A. Allen

Stress Less by Don Colbert, MD

Managing Your Emotions by Joyce Meyer

The Preacher's Outline & Sermon Bible – New International Version

www.healthline.com

BibleGateway.com

Scriptures marked ESV are taken from the THE HOLY BIBLE, ENGLISH STANDARD VERSION (ESV): Scriptures taken from THE HOLY BIBLE, ENGLISH STANDARD

- Amplified Bible
- Scriptures marked AMP are taken from the AMPLIFIED BIBLE (AMP): Scripture taken from the AMPLIFIED® BIBLE, Copyright © 1954, 1958, 1962, 1964, 1965, 1987 by the Lockman Foundation Used by Permission. (www.Lockman.org)
- KJV

Scriptures marked KJV are taken from the KING JAMES VERSION (KJV): KING JAMES VERSION, public domain.

- NKJV

Scriptures marked NKJV are taken from the NEW KING JAMES VERSION (NKJV): Scripture taken from the NEW KING JAMES VERSION®. Copyright© 1982 by Thomas Nelson, Inc. Used by permission. All rights reserved

Gotquestions.com

Biblehub.com

CHAPTER 1 HOW DEEP IS GOD'S WORD IN YOUR HEART?

Mark 4:1-9 in the NIV, let me explain some of the words what they mean.

Let me explain some of the words what they mean.

Farmer is Jesus or a teacher or preacher sharing God's promises.

Seed is the word of God.

Bird represents Satan.

Soil represents life here on earth and emotional health.

Grain means abundance, life, and spiritual fertility.

In Mark 4:1-9, in the NIV it reads:

[1] Again Jesus began to teach by the lake. The crowd that gathered around him was so large that he got into a boat and sat in it out on the lake, while all the people were along the shore at the water's edge.

[2] He taught them many things by parables, and in his teaching said:

[3] "Listen! A farmer went out to sow his seed.

[4] As he was scattering the seed, some fell along the path, and the birds came and ate it up.

[5] Some fell on rocky places, where it did not have much soil.

It sprang up quickly, because the soil was shallow.

⁶ But when the sun came up, the plants were scorched, and they withered because they had no root.

⁷ Other seed fell among <u>thorns,</u> which grew up and choked the plants, so that they did not bear grain.

⁸ Still other seed fell on <u>good soil</u>. It came up, grew and produced a crop, some multiplying thirty, some sixty, some a hundred times."

⁹ Then Jesus said, "Whoever has ears to hear, let them hear."

Jesus told Martha about listening in Luke 10:38-42, NIV, it reads:

³⁸ As Jesus and his disciples were on their way, he came to a village where a woman named Martha opened her home to him.

³⁹ She had a sister called Mary, who sat at the Lord's feet listening to what he said.

⁴⁰ But Martha was distracted by all the preparations that had to be made. She came to him and asked, "Lord, don't you care that my sister has left me to do the work by myself? Tell her to help me!"

⁴¹ "Martha, Martha," the Lord answered, "you are worried and upset about many things,

⁴² but few things are needed—or indeed only one. Mary has chosen what is better, and it will not be taken away from her

So, there are four types of soils that represent the heart of a person. Only the good soil produced the fruit of the spirit.

The hard soil was a hardening of the heart. The seed could not penetrate because of the soil not being soft and tender. Therefore, the devil came by and snatched the seed so it could not enter the heart. Remember, the bird represents the devil.

Jesus' heart is very grieved when a person's heart is hard and lacks understanding.

In Psalm 51:10-12, NIV, it reads:

¹⁰ Create in me a pure heart, O God, and renew a steadfast spirit within me.

¹¹ Do not cast me from your presence or take your Holy Spirit from me.

¹² Restore to me the joy of your salvation and grant me a willing spirit, to sustain me

In Mark 3:1-5, ESV reads...

¹ Again he entered the synagogue, and a man was there with a withered hand.

² And they watched Jesus, to see whether he would heal him on the Sabbath, so that they might accuse him.

³ And he said to the man with the withered hand, "Come here."

⁴ And he said to them, "Is it lawful on the Sabbath to do good or to do harm, to save life or to kill?" But they were silent.

⁵ And he looked around at them with anger, grieved at their hardness of heart, and said to the man, "Stretch out your hand." He stretched it out, and his hand was restored.

Jesus knew they all had a hard heart and the Word of God was not in them. Jesus only wants to give believers a new, clean, and soft heart.

Ezekiel 36:26-27, ESV states:

²⁶ I will give you a new heart and put a new spirit in you; I will remove from you your heart of stone and give you a heart of flesh.

²⁷ And I will put my Spirit in you and move you to follow my decrees and be careful to keep my laws.

The heart of flesh means to allow the Holy Spirit to work inwardly. God only wants to soften your heart so his Word can give you knowledge and wisdom so you can have a healthy soul.

The Bible explains in Ecclesiastes 8:1, and 7:11, NLT.

[1] How wonderful to be wise, to analyze and interpret things. Wisdom lights up a person's face, softening its harshness.

[11] Wisdom is even better when you have money. Both are a benefit as you go through life.

Luke 10:38-42, NIV reads:

God does not want you to have a wandering mindset. Our Heavenly Father wants your spiritual ears open to know the truth that can set you free.

It states in 2 Timothy 4:3-5, ESV

[3] For the time is coming when people will not endure sound teaching, but having itching ears they will accumulate for themselves teachers to suit their own passions,

[4] and will turn away from listening to the truth and wander off into myths.

[5] As for you, always be sober-minded, endure suffering, do the work of an evangelist, fulfill your ministry.

Now listen to an easier translation 2 Timothy 4:3-5, NLT

[3] For a time is coming when people will no longer listen to sound and wholesome teaching. They will follow their own desires and will look for teachers who will tell them whatever their itching ears want to hear.

[4] They will reject the truth and chase after myths.

[5] But you should keep a clear mind in every situation. Don't be afraid of suffering for the Lord. Work at telling others the Good News, and fully carry out the ministry God has given you.

All believers have the responsibility to share the love of God. God does not want anyone to be troubled and have a hard heart. His Word only brings blessing and benefits in our life.

Proverbs 28:14, NIV

¹⁴ Blessed are those who fear to do wrong, but the stubborn are headed for serious trouble.

The fear of the Lord is instruction of wisdom. It means to respect God, to obey God and to worship God. All believers need to honor our Lord and Savior.

Proverbs 1:2-7 and Proverbs 2:1-10 in the NLT is full of word of wisdom which says

² Their purpose is to teach people wisdom and discipline, to help them understand the insights of the wise.
³ Their purpose is to teach people to live disciplined and successful lives, to help them do what is right, just, and fair.
⁴ These proverbs will give insight to the simple, knowledge and discernment to the young.
⁵ Let the wise listen to these proverbs and become even wiser. Let those with understanding receive guidance
⁶ by exploring the meaning in these proverbs and parables, the words of the wise and their riddles.
⁷ Fear of the Lord is the foundation of true knowledge, but fools despise wisdom and discipline.

¹ My child, listen to what I say, and treasure my commands.
² Tune your ears to wisdom, and concentrate on understanding.
³ Cry out for insight, and ask for understanding.
⁴ Search for them as you would for silver; seek them like hidden treasures.
⁵ Then you will understand what it means to fear the Lord, and you will gain knowledge of God.
⁶ For the Lord grants wisdom! From his mouth come knowledge and understanding.
⁷ He grants a treasure of common sense to the honest. He is a shield to those who walk with integrity.
⁸ He guards the paths of the just and protects those who are faithful to him.

⁹Then you will understand what is right, just, and fair, and you will find the right way to go.
¹⁰For wisdom will enter your heart, and knowledge will fill you with joy.

God's word will go deeper into your heart as you get off the hard path and walk in the godly path. The Holy Spirit will heal you from a wandering worried mind.

God wants all believers to be happy and filled with joy. Let me walk you through Psalms 119, NLT that will lead you to a path of blessing.

Psalms 119:1-3, NLT

¹Joyful are people of integrity, who follow the instructions of the Lord.
²Joyful are those who obey his laws and search for him with all their hearts.
³They do not compromise with evil, and they walk only in his paths.

As you walk in a godly path, God's word will bless you as you apply His word. James 1:19-25, NIV states:

¹⁹My dear brothers and sisters, take note of this: Everyone should be quick to listen, slow to speak and slow to become angry,
²⁰because human anger does not produce the righteousness that God desires.
²¹Therefore, get rid of all moral filth and the evil that is so prevalent and humbly accept the word planted in you, which can save you.
²²Do not merely listen to the word, and so deceive yourselves. Do what it says.
²³Anyone who listens to the word but does not do what it says is like someone who looks at his face in a mirror
²⁴and, after looking at himself, goes away and immediately forgets what he looks like.

²⁵ But whoever looks intently into the perfect law that gives freedom, and continues in it—not forgetting what they have heard, but doing it—they will be blessed in what they do.

For additional reading, I hope you can make time to read Deuteronomy 28 and Matthew 5 to see and meditate on His blessings.

Psalms 119:8-12, NLT tells us...

⁸ I will obey your decrees. Please don't give up on me!
⁹ How can a young person stay pure? By obeying your word.
¹⁰ I have tried hard to find you—don't let me wander from your commands.
¹¹ I have hidden your word in my heart, that I might not sin against you.
¹² I praise you, O Lord; teach me your decrees.

David knew Jesus was the true vine and he long to stay connected to Jesus. He did not want to have a wandering mind. David wanted the word of God to sink in his heart. David was hungry for deep spiritual food. The mind reflects what sinks in your heart. That is the reason why you need to put on the attitude of Jesus. John 15:1-8, NLT explains about the true vine. It reads:

¹ "I am the true grapevine, and my Father is the gardener.

² He cuts off every branch of mine that doesn't produce fruit, and he prunes the branches that do bear fruit so they will produce even more.

³ You have already been pruned and purified by the message I have given you.

⁴ Remain in me, and I will remain in you. For a branch cannot produce fruit if it is severed from the vine, and you cannot be fruitful unless you remain in me.

⁵ "Yes, I am the vine; you are the branches. Those who remain in me, and I in them, will produce much fruit. For

apart from me you can do nothing.

⁶ Anyone who does not remain in me is thrown away like a useless branch and withers. Such branches are gathered into a pile to be burned. ⁷ But if you remain in me and my words remain in you, you may ask for anything you want, and it will be granted!

⁸ When you produce much fruit, you are my true disciples. This brings great glory to my Father.

God only wants you to have good soil to produce the fruit of the Spirit. Galatians 5:22-23, ESV speaks on the fruit which says:

²² But the fruit of the Spirit is love, joy, peace, patience, kindness, goodness, faithfulness,

²³ gentleness, self-control; against such there is no law.

Let's think of the opposite of good ripe fruit from rotten fruit:

Love vs Hate

Joy vs Sadness

Peace vs Chaos

Patience vs Impatience

Kindness vs Meanness

Goodness vs Evil Doing

Faithfulness vs Unfaithfulness

Gentleness vs Roughness

Self-Control vs Lack of Self Control

Remember the word of God is the seed. The seed contains the germ which pertains to a believer's spiritual growth. Germination means the process of something developing.

Are you being molded into God's image? The word of God transforms us. It tells us in 2 Corinthians 5:17, ESV states...

17 Therefore, if anyone is in Christ, he is a new creation. The old has passed away; behold, the new has come "

The Bible says a believer is wise when they apply God's promises. Matthew 7:24-27, NIV reads:

24 Therefore everyone who hears these words of mine and puts them into practice is like a wise man who built his house on the rock.

25 The rain came down, the streams rose, and the winds blew and beat against that house; yet it did not fall, because it had its foundation on the rock.

26 But everyone who hears these words of mine and does not put them into practice is like a foolish man who built his house on sand.

27 The rain came down, the streams rose, and the winds blew and beat against that house, and it fell with a great crash.

God is giving an illustration of a house you live in, but it pertains to your body which is what the Holy Spirit lives in.

2 Corinthians 5:1 Worldwide English Bible explains...

¹For we know that if the earthly house of our tent is dissolved, we have a building from God, a house not made with hands, eternal, in the heavens.

We will get a glorified body. In 1 Corinthians 15:40-42 NLT, it reads...

40 There are also bodies in the heavens and bodies on the earth. The glory of the heavenly bodies is different from the glory of the earthly bodies.

41 The sun has one kind of glory, while the moon and stars each have another kind. And even the stars differ from each other in their glory.

42 It is the same way with the resurrection of the dead. Our earthly bodies are planted in the ground when we die, but they will be raised to live forever.

Our body is the house in which our spirit lives in here on earth. When that house is destroyed, God will give us another house. That house is not made by man's hands. But God made it. It will last forever in Heaven.

The main point is when a believer builds his or her life on the Word of God, and has a strong foundation on the Rock, believers will not cave in and sink inwardly. When you allow God to be your rock, He will make you strong, solid, and stable within as you let the word reach your heart like David. Mental and emotional stress destroys the body Psalms 18:1-6, NLT says:

> [1]For we know that if the tent that is our earthly home is destroyed, we have a building from God, a house not made with hands, eternal in the heavens.
>
> [2] For in this tent we groan, longing to put on our heavenly dwelling,
>
> [3] if indeed by putting it on we may not be found naked.
>
> [4] For while we are still in this tent, we groan, being burdened—not that we would be unclothed, but that we would be further clothed, so that what is mortal may be swallowed up by life.
>
> [5] He who has prepared us for this very thing is God, who has given us the Spirit as a guarantee.
>
> [6] So we are always of good courage. We know that while we are at home in the body we are away from the Lord

God's ears are wide open to hear your cry. God wants no one to wander away from His promises. Read all the scriptures below to get a better understanding.

Psalms 119:21, NLT

> [21] You rebuke the arrogant; those who wander from your commands are cursed.

Psalms 119:25, NLT

> [25] I lie in the dust; revive me by your word.

Psalms 119:28, NLT

> [28] I weep with sorrow; encourage me by your word.

Psalms 119:37, NLT

> [37] Turn my eyes from worthless things, and give me life through your word.

Psalms 119:50, NLT

⁵⁰ Your promise revives me; it comforts me in all my troubles

People who stray away from God's commands will not experience God's blessings. Believers are to love God's commands like David. It gives us a sense of direction in life, sense of security, and peace of mind.

Psalms 119:47-48 NLT

⁴⁷ How I delight in your commands! How I love them!
⁴⁸ I honor and love your commands. I meditate on your decrees.

God's word lifts your spirit up. It helps to repair you, recharges you, renews you, and rejuvenates you.

Psalms 119:105 NLT

¹⁰⁵ Your word is a lamp to guide my feet and a light for my path.

Psalms 119:165, NLT

¹⁶⁵ Those who love your instructions have great peace and do not stumble.

Satan loves to plant evil seeds of doubt and unbelief. I pray you do not let doubt creep in your mind and you do not let your mind wander off of the Word of God.

Mark 11:22-25, NLT reads

²² Then Jesus said to the disciples, "Have faith in God.

²³ I tell you the truth, you can say to this mountain, 'May you be lifted up and thrown into the sea,' and it will happen. But you must really believe it will happen and have no doubt in your heart.

²⁴ I tell you, you can pray for anything, and if you believe that you've received it, it will be yours.

²⁵ But when you are praying, first forgive anyone you are

holding a grudge against, so that your Father in heaven will forgive your sins, too

God only asks for believers to make up their mind and expect Him to answer their prayer. James 1:2-7, NLT explains:

² Dear brothers and sisters, when troubles of any kind come your way, consider it an opportunity for great joy.

³ For you know that when your faith is tested, your endurance has a chance to grow.

⁴ So let it grow, for when your endurance is fully developed, you will be perfect and complete, needing nothing.

⁵ If you need wisdom, ask our generous God, and he will give it to you. He will not rebuke you for asking.

⁶ But when you ask him, be sure that your faith is in God alone. Do not waver, for a person with divided loyalty is as unsettled as a wave of the sea that is blown and tossed by the wind.

⁷ Such people should not expect to receive anything from the Lord

Maybe your mind is wandering and thinking; "when will life gets easier and less chaotic?" The answer can be found in God's Word. Believers need to stay alert and stand firm knowing God will lighten all of the burden in life. 1 Peter 5:8-9, NLT reads:

⁸ Stay alert! Watch out for your great enemy, the devil. He prowls around like a roaring lion, looking for someone to devour.

⁹ Stand firm against him, and be strong in your faith. Remember that your family of believers all over the world is going through the same kind of suffering you are.

Matthew 11:28-30, NLT tells us:

²⁸ Then Jesus said, "Come to me, all of you who are weary and carry heavy burdens, and I will give you rest.

^{29} Take my yoke upon you. Let me teach you, because I am humble and gentle at heart, and you will find rest for your souls.

^{30} For my yoke is easy to bear, and the burden I give you is light.

Mark 4:9-20, NLT says:

^{9} Then he said, "Anyone with ears to hear should listen and understand."

^{10} Later, when Jesus was alone with the twelve disciples and with the others who were gathered around, they asked him what the parables meant.

^{11} He replied, "You are permitted to understand the secret of the Kingdom of God. But I use parables for everything I say to outsiders,

^{12} so that the Scriptures might be fulfilled: When they see what I do, they will learn nothing. When they hear what I say, they will not understand. Otherwise, they will turn to me and be forgiven

^{13} Then Jesus said to them, "If you can't understand the meaning of this parable, how will you understand all the other parables?

^{14} The farmer plants seed by taking God's word to others.

^{15} The seed that fell on the footpath represents those who hear the message, only to have Satan come at once and take it away.

^{16} The seed on the rocky soil represents those who hear the message and immediately receive it with joy.

^{17} But since they don't have deep roots, they don't last long. They fall away as soon as they have problems or are persecuted for believing God's word.

^{18} The seed that fell among the thorns represents others who hear God's word,

¹⁹ but all too quickly the message is crowded out by the worries of this life, the lure of wealth, and the desire for other things, so no fruit is produced.

²⁰ And the seed that fell on good soil represents those who hear and accept God's word and produce a harvest of thirty, sixty, or even a hundred times as much as had been planted!

Life will be easier and less complicated as a person lets the Word of God penetrate in their heart. The hard path represents a hard heart that has no roots and the devil stolen the word. God only wants to soften your heart to bless believers with peace of mind and a calm peaceful heart.

In Mark 4:23-25, NLT, it reads..

²³ Anyone with ears to hear should listen and understand."

²⁴ Then he added, "Pay close attention to what you hear. The closer you listen, the more understanding you will be given and you will receive even more.

²⁵ To those who listen to my teaching, more understanding will be given. But for those who are not listening, even what little understanding they have will be taken away from them."

The Bible tells us in Romans 10:17, NKJV, So, then faith comes by hearing and hearing by the word of God.

God's word can crush the hardness of a person hard heart according to the scripture found in Jeremiah 23:29, NLT which says, ²⁹ Does not my word burn like fire?" says the Lord. "Is it not like a mighty hammer that smashes a rock to pieces?"

If the seed does not touch your heart, it is impossible for a person to learn, grow, and mature spiritually. The evil false prophets would not listen to God. It tells us in Jeremiah 23:18, and 21-22, NLT:

¹⁸ "Have any of these prophets been in the Lord's presence to

hear what he is really saying? Has even one of them cared enough to listen?

²¹ "I have not sent these prophets, yet they run around claiming to speak for me. I have given them no message, yet they go on prophesying.
²² If they had stood before me and listened to me, they would have spoken my words, and they would have turned my people from their evil ways and deeds.

By applying God's promises, He will give you peace of mind when you allow the Word of God to take root in your heart. In Philippians 4:6-9, NLT it reads:

⁶ Don't worry about anything; instead, pray about everything. Tell God what you need, and thank him for all he has done.

⁷ Then you will experience God's peace, which exceeds anything we can understand. His peace will guard your hearts and minds as you live in Christ Jesus.

⁸ And now, dear brothers and sisters, one final thing. Fix your thoughts on what is true, and honorable, and right, and pure, and lovely, and admirable. Think about things that are excellent and worthy of praise.

⁹ Keep putting into practice all you learned and received from me—everything you heard from me and saw me doing. Then the God of peace will be with you.

Jesus is called Wonderful, Counselor, Mighty God, Everlasting Father, Prince of Peace in Isaiah 9:6.

As you grow in knowledge, you will not fall into the same struggles over and over. You will experience God's goodness. 1 Peter 2:2, NIV, explains:

² Like newborn babies, crave pure spiritual milk, so that by it you may grow up in your salvation,

As a believer one must crave and desire the milk of God's word to grow up in his or her salvation.

The meaning of salvation is being saved from sin or evil and from danger or difficulty.

3 John verses 2, 3 and 4, in the NKJV, tells us:

> [2] Beloved, I pray that you may prosper in all things and be in health, just as your soul prospers.
>
> [3] For I rejoiced greatly when brethren came and testified of the truth *that is* in you, just as you walk in the truth.
>
> [4] I have no greater joy than to hear that my children walk in truth.

Are you walking in the truth? God wants all believers to be spiritually mature to live out a victorious life on earth.

Just as Paul loved and cared for the believers in church, God cares for his sons and daughters and wants to give them love and support, when preachers, teachers, or evangelists share God's promises. Colossians 1:7-14, 24-25, 28, 2:1-3, ESV reads:

> [7] You learned about the Good News from Epaphras, our beloved co-worker. He is Christ's faithful servant, and he is helping us on your behalf.
>
> [8] He has told us about the love for others that the Holy Spirit has given you.
>
> [9] So we have not stopped praying for you since we first heard about you. We ask God to give you complete knowledge of his will and to give you spiritual wisdom and understanding.
>
> [10] Then the way you live will always honor and please the Lord, and your lives will produce every kind of good fruit. All the while, you will grow as you learn to know God better and better.
>
> [11] We also pray that you will be strengthened with all his glorious power so you will have all the endurance and patience you need. May you be filled with joy,
>
> [12] always thanking the Father. He has enabled you to share

in the inheritance that belongs to his people, who live in the light.

¹³ For he has rescued us from the kingdom of darkness and transferred us into the Kingdom of his dear Son,

¹⁴ who purchased our freedom and forgave our sins.

²⁴ I am glad when I suffer for you in my body, for I am participating in the sufferings of Christ that continue for his body, the church.

²⁵ God has given me the responsibility of serving his church by proclaiming his entire message to you.

²⁸ So we tell others about Christ, warning everyone and teaching everyone with all the wisdom God has given us. We want to present them to God, perfect[g] in their relationship to Christ.

₁ I want you to know how much I have agonized for you and for the church at Laodicea, and for many other believers who have never met me personally.

² I want them to be encouraged and knit together by strong ties of love. I want them to have complete confidence that they understand God's mysterious plan, which is Christ himself.

³ In him lie hidden all the treasures of wisdom and knowledge.

The Word of God can teach and train all believers to get their life in spiritual order. 2 Timothy 3:16, NLT reads:

¹⁶ All Scripture is inspired by God and is useful to teach us what is true and to make us realize what is wrong in our lives. It corrects us when we are wrong and teaches us to do what is right.

God desires for all believers to gain knowledge and apply the wisdom to their life.

Some people in Israel had hardened their hearts, but God

always encouraged them even though they worshipped idols. Their hearts were unplowed and God's word could not reach their heart.

Hosea 10:12, NLT reads,

> 12 I said, 'Plant the good seeds of righteousness, and you will harvest a crop of love. Plow up the hard ground of your hearts, for now is the time to seek the Lord, that he may come and shower righteousness upon you

Jesus came to save the world not judge the world. Jesus will forgive a believer's hard heart. John 12:44-48, ESV says:

> 44 And Jesus cried out and said, "Whoever believes in me, believes not in me but in him who sent me.

> 45 And whoever sees me sees him who sent me.

> 46 I have come into the world as light, so that whoever believes in me may not remain in darkness.

> 47 If anyone hears my words and does not keep them, I do not judge him; for I did not come to judge the world but to save the world.

> 48 The one who rejects me and does not receive my words has a judge; the word that I have spoken will judge him on the last day.

Mark 4:9, 13-25, NLT tells us:

> 9 Then he said, "Anyone with ears to hear should listen and understand.

> 13 Then Jesus said to them, "If you can't understand the meaning of this parable, how will you understand all the other parables?

> 14 The farmer plants seed by taking God's word to others.

> 15 The seed that fell on the footpath represents those who hear the message, only to have satan come at once and take it away.

16 The seed on the rocky soil represents those who hear the message and immediately receive it with joy.

17 But since they don't have deep roots, they don't last long. They fall away as soon as they have problems or are persecuted for believing God's word.

18 The seed that fell among the thorns represents others who hear God's word,

19 but all too quickly the message is crowded out by the worries of this life, the lure of wealth, and the desire for other things, so no fruit is produced.

20 And the seed that fell on good soil represents those who hear and accept God's word and produce a harvest of thirty, sixty, or even a hundred times as much as had been planted!

21 Then Jesus asked them, "Would anyone light a lamp and then put it under a basket or under a bed? Of course not! A lamp is placed on a stand, where its light will shine.

22 For everything that is hidden will eventually be brought into the open, and every secret will be brought to light.

23 Anyone with ears to hear should listen and understand."

24 Then he added, "Pay close attention to what you hear. The closer you listen, the more understanding you will be given and you will receive even more.

25 To those who listen to my teaching, more understanding will be given. But for those who are not listening, even what little understanding they have will be taken away from them.

Remember the soil represents life here on earth and emotional health. God cares about the issues of your heart.

The second soil is the **rocky heart soil** which had some roots but a short life. The hot sun killed the seed. This person heart is a rootless heart which leads to a superficial life. This person has a confused mind. God is not the author of confusion.

He is a God of order and not chaos.

The Holy Spirit wants his sons and daughters rooted and grounded in his promises. Let Paul's prayer speak to your heart. In Ephesians 3:14-19, NLT, it reads:

[14] When I think of all this, I fall to my knees and pray to the Father,

[15] the Creator of everything in heaven and on earth.

[16] I pray that from his glorious, unlimited resources he will empower you with inner strength through his Spirit.

[17] Then Christ will make his home in your hearts as you trust in him. Your roots will grow down into God's love and keep you strong.

[18] And may you have the power to understand, as all God's people should, how wide, how long, how high, and how deep his love is.

[19] May you experience the love of Christ, though it is too great to understand fully. Then you will be made complete with all the fullness of life and power that comes from God.

God is the:

Author of Life – Acts 3:15, NIV

Breath of Life – Genesis 2:7, ESV

Tree of Life – Genesis 2:7-10, ESV

Jesus is the:

Bread of Life – John 6:35, ESV

Foundation of Life – Matthew 7:24-27, NIV

Fountain of Life – John 4:1-14, NIV

Light of Life – John 8:12, NIV

Water of Life – Revelations 22:1, NIV

Resurrection of Life – John 11:1-15, NIV

Jesus is the bread of life that satisfies your spiritual hunger

The Bible tell us in Acts 3:13-15, NLT God is the author of life which reads:

¹³ For it is the God of Abraham, Isaac, and Jacob—the God of all our ancestors—who has brought glory to his servant Jesus by doing this. This is the same Jesus whom you handed over and rejected before Pilate, despite Pilate's decision to release him.

¹⁴ You rejected this holy, righteous one and instead demanded the release of a murderer.

¹⁵ You killed the author of life, but God raised him from the dead. And we are witnesses of this fact!

John 6:29-40, NLT reads:

²⁹ Jesus told them, "This is the only work God wants from you: Believe in the one he has sent."

³⁰ They answered, "Show us a miraculous sign if you want us to believe in you. What can you do?

³¹ After all, our ancestors ate manna while they journeyed through the wilderness! The Scriptures say, 'Moses gave them bread from heaven to eat.'

³² Jesus said, "I tell you the truth, Moses didn't give you bread from heaven. My Father did. And now he offers you the true bread from heaven.

³³ The true bread of God is the one who comes down from heaven and gives life to the world."

³⁴ "Sir," they said, "give us that bread every day."

³⁵ Jesus replied, "I am the bread of life. Whoever comes to me will never be hungry again. Whoever believes in me will never be thirsty.

³⁶ But you haven't believed in me even though you have seen me.

37 However, those the Father has given me will come to me, and I will never reject them.

38 For I have come down from heaven to do the will of God who sent me, not to do my own will.

39 And this is the will of God, that I should not lose even one of all those he has given me, but that I should raise them up at the last day.

40 For it is my Father's will that all who see his Son and believe in him should have eternal life. I will raise them up at the last day."

God can give you a fulfilled life. He does not want your heart to stay rocky or your mind to be confused. Ephesians 4:17-19, NLT reads:

17 With the Lord's authority I say this: Live no longer as the Gentiles do, for they are hopelessly confused.

18 Their minds are full of darkness; they wander far from the life God gives because they have closed their minds and hardened their hearts against him.

19 They have no sense of shame. They live for lustful pleasure and eagerly practice every kind of impurity.

The rocky heart soil lacks spiritual nourishment. Jesus does not want a believer to drift away. In Hebrews 2:1, ESV it says:

1Therefore we must pay much closer attention to what we have heard, lest we drift away from it.

God wants to speak into your life and open up your mind of understanding. Jesus can give you the Spirit of truth. It reads in Luke 24:44-49, ESV:

44 Then he said to them, "These are my words that I spoke to you while I was still with you, that everything written about me in the Law of Moses and the Prophets and the Psalms must be fulfilled."

45 Then he opened their minds to understand the Scriptures,

46 and said to them, "Thus it is written, that the Christ should suffer and on the third day rise from the dead,

47 and that repentance for the forgiveness of sins should be proclaimed in his name to all nations, beginning from Jerusalem.

48 You are witnesses of these things.

49 And behold, I am sending the promise of my Father upon you. But stay in the city until you are clothed with power from on high.

This is where Jesus appeared to his disciples after being resurrected from the dead. One of Jesus' disciples had doubt in his heart. The Bible states in John 20:24-29, NIV:

24 Now Thomas (also known as Didymus), one of the Twelve, was not with the disciples when Jesus came.

25 So the other disciples told him, "We have seen the Lord!" But he said to them, "Unless I see the nail marks in his hands and put my finger where the nails were, and put my hand into his side, I will not believe."

26 A week later his disciples were in the house again, and Thomas was with them. Though the doors were locked, Jesus came and stood among them and said, "Peace be with you!"

27 Then he said to Thomas, "Put your finger here; see my hands. Reach out your hand and put it into my side. Stop doubting and believe."

28 Thomas said to him, "My Lord and my God!"

29 Then Jesus told him, "Because you have seen me, you have believed; blessed are those who have not seen and yet have believed

God does not want doubt to enter your heart. Jesus is the Spirit of truth. In 1 John 4:1-10, NLT clarifies it very clearly which says:

> [1]Dear friends, do not believe everyone who claims to speak by the Spirit. You must test them to see if the spirit they have comes from God. For there are many false prophets in the world.
>
> [2] This is how we know if they have the Spirit of God: If a person claiming to be a prophet acknowledges that Jesus Christ came in a real body, that person has the Spirit of God.
>
> [3] But if someone claims to be a prophet and does not acknowledge the truth about Jesus, that person is not from God. Such a person has the spirit of the Antichrist, which you heard is coming into the world and indeed is already here.
>
> [4] But you belong to God, my dear children. You have already won a victory over those people, because the Spirit who lives in you is greater than the spirit who lives in the world.
>
> [5] Those people belong to this world, so they speak from the world's viewpoint, and the world listens to them.
>
> [6] But we belong to God, and those who know God listen to us. If they do not belong to God, they do not listen to us. That is how we know if someone has the Spirit of truth or the spirit of deception.
>
> [7] Dear friends, let us continue to love one another, for love comes from God. Anyone who loves is a child of God and knows God.
>
> [8] But anyone who does not love does not know God, for God is love.
>
> [9] God showed how much he loved us by sending his one and only Son into the world so that we might have eternal life through him.
>
> [10] This is real love—not that we loved God, but that he loved us and sent his Son as a sacrifice to take away our sins.

God can bless believers when they are spiritually hot and fully committed to hear, understand, and comprehend his message. Revelation 3:15-16, NLT tells us:

> ¹⁵ I know all the things you do, that you are neither hot nor cold. I wish that you were one or the other!

> ¹⁶ But since you are like lukewarm water, neither hot nor cold, I will spit you out of my mouth!

There are three anointed spirits (manifestations of the Holy Spirit's nature in us) a believer must have to stay spiritually hot and hear from God. The letter H stands for a Humble Spirit. The letter O stands for an Obedient Spirit and the T stands for a Teachable Spirit.

A humble spirit has a low view of one's importance. A proud spirit shows a high opinion of self. 1 Peter 5:5-11, NLT explains:

> ⁵ In the same way, you who are younger must accept the authority of the elders. And all of you, dress yourselves in humility as you relate to one another, for "God opposes the proud but gives grace to the humble."

> ⁶ So humble yourselves under the mighty power of God, and at the right time he will lift you up in honor.

> ⁷ Give all your worries and cares to God, for he cares about you.

> ⁸ Stay alert! Watch out for your great enemy, the devil. He prowls around like a roaring lion, looking for someone to devour.

> ⁹ Stand firm against him, and be strong in your faith. Remember that your family of believers all over the world is going through the same kind of suffering you are.

> ¹⁰ In his kindness God called you to share in his eternal glory by means of Christ Jesus. So after you have suffered a little while, he will restore, support, and strengthen you, and he will place you on a firm foundation.

> ¹¹ All power to him forever! Amen.

The favor of God is divine kindness. He gives all believers godly ability to do the impossible. God's grace give blessing we do not even deserve. Psalms 69:32-33, NLT tells us:

> ³²The humble will see their God at work and be glad. Let all who seek God's help be encouraged.
>
> ³³ For the Lord hears the cries of the needy; he does not despise his imprisoned people.

The meaning of despise in the Bible means to look down on with disrespect. God will not overlook or ignore the cries of his people who are oppressed. The meaning of oppressed means subject to harsh and authoritarian treatment.

No parents, police officers, political parties, joint chiefs, managers, lawyers, judges, preachers, or teachers has 100% righteous authority if they do not hear from God who has supreme authority. He is the sovereign God. God wants every leader to be humble and respect others. Proverbs 22:4, NLT says:

> ⁴ True humility and fear of the Lord lead to riches, honor, and long life.

The fear of God means a sense of respect and submission to deity. Deity means the creator and supreme being.

James 3:13-18, NIV reads:

> ¹³ Who is wise and understanding among you? Let them show it by their good life, by deeds done in the humility that comes from wisdom.
>
> ¹⁴ But if you harbor bitter envy and selfish ambition in your hearts, do not boast about it or deny the truth.
>
> ¹⁵ Such "wisdom" does not come down from heaven but is earthly, unspiritual, demonic.
>
> ¹⁶ For where you have envy and selfish ambition, there you find disorder and every evil practice.
>
> ¹⁷ But the wisdom that comes from heaven is first of all pure; then peace-loving, considerate, submissive, full of

mercy and good fruit, impartial and sincere.

¹⁸ Peacemakers who sow in peace reap a harvest of righteousness.

A great humble leader has the attitude of Jesus and imitates Jesus' humility.

Philippians 2:1-11, NLT reads:

> ¹Is there any encouragement from belonging to Christ? Any comfort from his love? Any fellowship together in the Spirit? Are your hearts tender and compassionate?
> ² Then make me truly happy by agreeing wholeheartedly with each other, loving one another, and working together with one mind and purpose.
> ³ Don't be selfish; don't try to impress others. Be humble, thinking of others as better than yourselves.
> ⁴ Don't look out only for your own interests, but take an interest in others, too.
> ⁵ You must have the same attitude that Christ Jesus had.
> ⁶ Though he was God, he did not think of equality with God as something to cling to.
> ⁷ Instead, he gave up his divine privileges; he took the humble position of a slave and was born as a human being. When he appeared in human form,
> ⁸he humbled himself in obedience to God and died a criminal's death on a cross.
> ⁹ Therefore, God elevated him to the place of highest honor and gave him the name above all other names,
> ¹⁰ that at the name of Jesus every knee should bow, in heaven and on earth and under the earth,
> ¹¹ and every tongue declare that Jesus Christ is Lord, to the glory of God the Father.

God told the people in Israel to plow up their hard hearts. In Hosea 10:12, NLT, it reads:

> ¹² I said, 'Plant the good seeds of righteousness, and you

will harvest a crop of love. Plow up the hard ground of your hearts, for now is the time to seek the Lord, that he may come and shower righteousness upon you.

The people of Israel would not give up worshipping idols. Exodus 20:2-3 ESV, tells us:

² "I am the Lord your God, who brought you out of the land of Egypt, out of the house of slavery.

³ "You shall have no other gods before me

So, I pray you stay humble. The Bible says in Proverbs 11:2, ESV "When pride comes, then comes disgrace, but with the humble is wisdom".

Stay rooted in the Word and you will rise above your problems here on earth. Mark 4:9-20, NLT reads...

⁹ Then he said, "Anyone with ears to hear should listen and understand."

¹⁰ Later, when Jesus was alone with the twelve disciples and with the others who were gathered around, they asked him what the parables meant.

¹¹ He replied, "You are permitted to understand the secret of the Kingdom of God. But I use parables for everything I say to outsiders,

¹² so that the Scriptures might be fulfilled: When they see what I do, they will learn nothing. When they hear what I say, they will not understand. Otherwise, they will turn to me and be forgiven.

¹³ Then Jesus said to them, "If you can't understand the meaning of this parable, how will you understand all the other parables?

¹⁴ The farmer plants seed by taking God's word to others.

¹⁵ The seed that fell on the footpath represents those who hear the message, only to have Satan come at once and take it away.

¹⁶ The seed on the rocky soil represents those who hear the message and immediately receive it with joy.

¹⁷ But since they don't have deep roots, they don't last long. They fall away as soon as they have problems or are persecuted for believing God's word.

¹⁸ The seed that fell among the thorns represents others who hear God's word,

¹⁹ but all too quickly the message is crowded out by the worries of this life, the lure of wealth, and the desire for other things, so no fruit is produced.

²⁰ And the seed that fell on good soil represents those who hear and accept God's word and produce a harvest of thirty, sixty, or even a hundred times as much as had been planted

God wants all of his sons and daughters to listen deeply so his word benefits their life. Mark 4:23-25, NLT states:

²³ Anyone with ears to hear should listen and understand."

²⁴ Then he added, "Pay close attention to what you hear. The closer you listen, the more understanding you will be given and you will receive even more.

²⁵ To those who listen to my teaching, more understanding will be given. But for those who are not listening, even what little understanding they have will be taken away from them.

By staying spiritually hot the Holy Ghost fire will burn deeply in a believer's heart. When a believer listens, reads, studies and meditates on God's promises, it proves how much you love God. Hearing God's voice becomes easier when a believer keeps a humble attitude and an obedient spirit. The second letter in Hot is O and it stands for an Obedient Spirit.

In John 14:15-27, NLT explains:

¹⁵ "If you love me, obey my commandments.

16 And I will ask the Father, and he will give you another Advocate, who will never leave you.

17 He is the Holy Spirit, who leads into all truth. The world cannot receive him, because it isn't looking for him and doesn't recognize him. But you know him, because he lives with you now and later will be in you.

18 No, I will not abandon you as orphans—I will come to you.

19 Soon the world will no longer see me, but you will see me. Since I live, you also will live.

20 When I am raised to life again, you will know that I am in my Father, and you are in me, and I am in you.

21 Those who accept my commandments and obey them are the ones who love me. And because they love me, my Father will love them. And I will love them and reveal myself to each of them."

22 Judas (not Judas Iscariot, but the other disciple with that name) said to him, "Lord, why are you going to reveal yourself only to us and not to the world at large?"

23 Jesus replied, "All who love me will do what I say. My Father will love them, and we will come and make our home with each of them.

24 Anyone who doesn't love me will not obey me. And remember, my words are not my own. What I am telling you is from the Father who sent me.

25 I am telling you these things now while I am still with you.

26 But when the Father sends the Advocate as my representative—that is, the Holy Spirit—he will teach you everything and will remind you of everything I have told you.

27 "I am leaving you with a gift—peace of mind and heart. And the peace I give is a gift the world cannot give. So, don't be troubled or afraid.

God reveals himself through the Word. Most people know if you do not add wood to a fire it will go out. 1 Thessalonians 5:16-19, NIV states:

16 Rejoice always,

17 pray continually,

18 give thanks in all circumstances; for this is God's will for you in Christ Jesus.

19 Do not quench the Spirit.

God does not want your spiritual fire to go out. In Luke 24:32, ESV, it reads:

32 They said to each other, "Did not our hearts burn within us while he talked to us on the road, while he opened to us the Scriptures?

Now let me paraphrase some of the story: One of God's disciples Cleopras and his friend were walking on the road Emmaus. Jesus was on the same road. Both disciples were very sad about the Lord's crucifixion. Jesus was the subject of their conversation. Jesus started to walk together with them both and neither of them recognized Jesus. In Luke 24:28-35, ESV it will explain the end of the story. It says:

28 So they drew near to the village to which they were going. He acted as if he were going farther,

29 but they urged him strongly, saying, "Stay with us, for it is toward evening and the day is now far spent." So he went in to stay with them.

30 When he was at table with them, he took the bread and blessed and broke it and gave it to them.

31 And their eyes were opened, and they recognized him. And he vanished from their sight.

32 They said to each other, "Did not our hearts burn within us while he talked to us on the road, while he opened to us the Scriptures?"

³³ And they rose that same hour and returned to Jerusalem. And they found the eleven and those who were with them gathered together,

³⁴ saying, "The Lord has risen indeed, and has appeared to Simon!"

³⁵ Then they told what had happened on the road, and how he was known to them in the breaking of the bread.

Simon named in the Hebrew means the one whom hears. Jesus knew he was not going to talk to death ears. Jesus changes Simon name to Peter because he had a spiritual transformation and heard from God which is called spiritual rock when this occurred. Peter's name in Hebrew means stone or rock. Now this is astonishing to me, because rock means truth. Jesus uses both names together in Matthew 16:13-18 NLT.These verses tell us:

¹³ When Jesus came to the region of Caesarea Philippi, he asked his disciples, "Who do people say that the Son of Man is?"

¹⁴ "Well," they replied, "some say John the Baptist, some say Elijah, and others say Jeremiah or one of the other prophets."

¹⁵ Then he asked them, "But who do you say I am?"

¹⁶ Simon Peter answered, "You are the Messiah, the Son of the living God."

¹⁷ Jesus replied, "You are blessed, Simon son of John, because my Father in heaven has revealed this to you. You did not learn this from any human being.

¹⁸ Now I say to you that you are Peter (which means 'rock'), and upon this rock I will build my church, and all the powers of hell will not conquer it.

So, both names together in verse 16 Simon Peter means the one whom hears the truth.

What Jesus was saying is that Peter was a small stone but would be a massive rock which would build God's Kingdom.

Peter was the first to confess Jesus as the Lords Messiah and Son of God. Peter's name may mean rock, but Jesus is our true rock. In 1 Corinthians 10:4, ESV, it reads:

> [4] and all drank the same spiritual drink. For they drank from the spiritual Rock that followed them, and the Rock was Christ.

Peter had an obedient spirit. The Bible says in Luke 5:1-11, NLT…

> [1] One day as Jesus was preaching on the shore of the Sea of Galilee, great crowds pressed in on him to listen to the word of God.
>
> [2] He noticed two empty boats at the water's edge, for the fishermen had left them and were washing their nets.
>
> [3] Stepping into one of the boats, Jesus asked Simon, its owner, to push it out into the water. So he sat in the boat and taught the crowds from there.
>
> [4] When he had finished speaking, he said to Simon, "Now go out where it is deeper, and let down your nets to catch some fish."
>
> [5] "Master," Simon replied, "we worked hard all last night and didn't catch a thing. But if you say so, I'll let the nets down again."
>
> [6] And this time their nets were so full of fish they began to tear!
>
> [7] A shout for help brought their partners in the other boat, and soon both boats were filled with fish and on the verge of sinking.
>
> [8] When Simon Peter realized what had happened, he fell to his knees before Jesus and said, "Oh, Lord, please leave me— I'm such a sinful man."
>
> [9] For he was awestruck by the number of fish they had caught, as were the others with him.
>
> [10] His partners, James and John, the sons of Zebedee, were

also amazed. Jesus replied to Simon, "Don't be afraid! From now on you'll be fishing for people!"

¹¹ And as soon as they landed, they left everything and followed Jesus.

Believers are blessed when they obey God. Deuteronomy 28:13-14, NIV, says:

¹³ The Lord will make you the head, not the tail. If you pay attention to the commands of the Lord your God that I give you this day and carefully follow them, you will always be at the top, never at the bottom.

¹⁴ Do not turn aside from any of the commands I give you today, to the right or to the left, following other gods and serving them.

Revelation 1:3, ESV reads:

Blessed is the one who reads aloud the words of this prophecy, and blessed are those who hear, and who keep what is written in it, for the time is near.

Now let me walk you through the Beatitudes. In Matthew 5:1-3, NIV, it says...

¹Now when Jesus saw the crowds, he went up on a mountainside and sat down. His disciples came to him,

² and he began to teach them.

³ "Blessed are the poor in spirit, for theirs is the kingdom of heaven.

To be blessed means to have spiritual joy and satisfaction that lasts regardless of conditions that carries one through pain, sorrow, loss, and grief. Being poor in spirit is not being financially poor, it means:

- To acknowledge our helplessness before God to meet our spiritual needs. Godly dependence is trusting God and not being mentally or emotionally stressed out. Proverbs 3:5-6, ESV says...

⁵ Trust in the Lord with all your heart, and do not lean on your own understanding.
⁶ In all your ways acknowledge him, and he will make straight your paths.

- It is acknowledging that the Holy Spirit can help us face life on this earth successfully and blesses all His sons and daughters. Jeremiah 17:7-10, ESV reads...

⁷ "Blessed is the man who trusts in the Lord,
  whose trust is the Lord.
⁸ He is like a tree planted by water, that sends out its roots by the stream, and does not fear when heat comes, for its leaves remain green, and is not anxious in the year of drought, for it does not cease to bear fruit."
⁹ The heart is deceitful above all things, and desperately sick; who can understand it?
¹⁰ "I the Lord search the heart and test the mind,
  to give every man according to his ways, according to the fruit of his deeds."

Ephesians 1:3, 7-8 reads:
³ Blessed be the God and Father of our Lord Jesus Christ, who has blessed us in Christ with every spiritual blessing in the heavenly places,
⁷ In him we have redemption through his blood, the forgiveness of our trespasses, according to the riches of his grace,
⁸ which he lavished upon us, in all wisdom and insight

Matthew 5:4-12, NIV reads:
⁴ Blessed are those who mourn, for they will be comforted.
⁵ Blessed are the meek, for they will inherit the earth.
⁶ Blessed are those who hunger and thirst for righteousness, for they will be filled.
⁷ Blessed are the merciful, for they will be shown mercy.

⁸ Blessed are the pure in heart, for they will see God.

⁹ Blessed are the peacemakers, for they will be called children of God.

¹⁰ Blessed are those who are persecuted because of righteousness,

for theirs is the kingdom of heaven.

¹¹ "Blessed are you when people insult you, persecute you and falsely say all kinds of evil against you because of me.

¹² Rejoice and be glad, because great is your reward in heaven, for in the same way they persecuted the prophets who were before you.

And in the NLT, the same passage reads:

⁴ God blesses those who mourn, for they will be comforted.

⁵ God blesses those who are humble, for they will inherit the whole earth.

⁶ God blesses those who hunger and thirst for justice, for they will be satisfied.

⁷ God blesses those who are merciful, for they will be shown mercy.

⁸ God blesses those whose hearts are pure, for they will see God.

⁹ God blesses those who work for peace, for they will be called the children of God.

¹⁰ God blesses those who are persecuted for doing right, for the Kingdom of Heaven is theirs.

¹¹ "God blesses you when people mock you and persecute you and lie about you and say all sorts of evil things against you because you are my followers.

¹² Be happy about it! Be very glad! For a great reward awaits you in heaven. And remember, the ancient prophets were persecuted in the same way.

Believers are too blessed to be stressed!

God's blessing is ultimately the process of rejuvenating every believer back to uplifting positive state of mind.

God only wants to shower blessings on your life. Life can be stressful, hard, hectic, and chaotic sometimes. I Hope you can memorize some scriptures below to help you cope with life wisely and successfully. Deuteronomy 28:2, ESV says:

And all these blessings shall come upon you and overtake you, if you obey the voice of the Lord your God.

Proverbs 16:20, ESV reads:

Whoever gives thought to the word will discover good, and blessed is he who trusts in the Lord.

2 Peter 1:3, ESV says:

[1]Simeon Peter, a servant and apostle of Jesus Christ, to those who have obtained a faith of equal standing with ours by the righteousness of our God and Savior Jesus Christ:

[2] May grace and peace be multiplied to you in the knowledge of God and of Jesus our Lord.

[3] His divine power has granted to us all things that pertain to life and godliness, through the knowledge of him who called us to his own glory and excellence,

Psalms 119:1-3, ESV reads:

[1]Blessed are those whose way is blameless, who walk in the law of the Lord!

[2] Blessed are those who keep his testimonies, who seek him with their whole heart,

[3] who also do no wrong, but walk in his ways!

Psalms 34:8-9, ESV says:

[8] Oh, taste and see that the Lord is good! Blessed is the man who takes refuge in him!

[9] Oh, fear the Lord, you his saints,

Mark 4:23-25, NLT reads...

[23] Anyone with ears to hear should listen and understand.

[24] Then he added, "Pay close attention to what you hear. The closer you listen, the more understanding you will be given and you will receive even more.

[25] To those who listen to my teaching, more understanding will be given. But for those who are not listening, even what little understanding they have will be taken away from them.

God wants all his sons and daughters to have more understanding and have deep roots of God's word in their heart. Mark 4:14-20, NLT says...

[14] The farmer plants seed by taking God's word to others.

[15] The seed that fell on the footpath represents those who hear the message, only to have Satan come at once and take it away.

[16] The seed on the rocky soil represents those who hear the message and immediately receive it with joy.

[17] But since they don't have deep roots, they don't last long. They fall away as soon as they have problems or are persecuted for believing God's word.

[18] The seed that fell among the thorns represents others who hear God's word,

[19] but all too quickly the message is crowded out by the worries of this life, the lure of wealth, and the desire for other things, so no fruit is produced.

[20] And the seed that fell on good soil represents those who hear and accept God's word and produce a harvest of thirty, sixty, or even a hundred times as much as had been planted!

The rocky heart soil had some roots and received the word with delight but had very short life. The hot sun killed the plant because of shallow soil. This person's heart is a rootless heart which leads to a confused mind. God is not the author of confusion. He is a God of order and not chaos. Ephesians 4:17-19, NLT, reads…

¹⁷ With the Lord's authority I say this: Live no longer as the Gentiles do, for they are hopelessly confused.

¹⁸ Their minds are full of darkness; they wander far from the life God gives because they have closed their minds and hardened their hearts against him.

¹⁹ They have no sense of shame. They live for lustful pleasure and eagerly practice every kind of impurity.

Proverbs 28:14, ESV explains about a rocky heart which reads:

¹⁴ Blessed is the one who fears the Lord[b] always, but whoever hardens his heart will fall into calamity.

The meaning of calamity is an event causing great and often sudden damage or distress or disaster. God does not want the believer to go through needless drama. John 10:10, NKJV says:

¹⁰ The thief does not come except to steal, and to kill, and to destroy. I have come that they may have life, and that they may have *it* more abundantly.

In order to be blessed and have an abundant life, one must be humble and stay spiritually hot. Remember as said earlier, the second letter in Hot is O which stands for an Obedient Spirit.

Obedience in the Hebrew means to hear, to listen, to give attention to, to understand, to submit, and to obey. There are spiritual benefits knowing God's word. It can put everlasting joy deep within your heart as you get stronger deeper roots. Psalms 19:7-11, NLT states:

⁷The instructions of the Lord are perfect, reviving the soul. The decrees of the Lord are trustworthy, making wise the simple.
⁸ The commandments of the Lord are right, bringing joy to the heart. The commands of the Lord are clear, giving insight for living.

⁹ Reverence for the Lord is pure, lasting forever. The laws of the Lord are true; each one is fair.

¹⁰ They are more desirable than gold, even the finest gold. They are sweeter than honey, even honey dripping from the comb.

¹¹ They are a warning to your servant, a great reward for those who <u>obey</u> them.

Now, two great rewards God gives is peace of mind and a sense of security. There are many more as you read the Bible. You will find nothing but blessings. Psalms 119:165, NLT says:

¹⁶⁵ Those who love your instructions have great peace and do not stumble.

Isaiah 32:18, NKJV reads...

¹⁸ My people will dwell in a peaceful habitation, In secure dwellings, and in quiet resting places,

Noah listened and obeyed God and rescued him and his family.

Genesis 6:5-9, NLT explains...

⁵ The Lord observed the extent of human wickedness on the earth, and he saw that everything they thought or imagined was consistently and totally evil.

⁶ So the Lord was sorry he had ever made them and put them on the earth. It broke his heart.

⁷ And the Lord said, "I will wipe this human race I have created from the face of the earth. Yes, and I will destroy every living thing—all the people, the large animals, the small animals that scurry along the ground, and even the birds of the sky. I am sorry I ever made them."

⁸ But Noah found favor with the Lord.

⁹ This is the account of Noah and his family. Noah was a righteous man, the only blameless person living on earth at the time, and he walked in close fellowship with God.

God told Noah to build a boat, because the earth was going to be destroyed by a flood. God promised to keep Noah and his family safe. Genesis 6:22, NLT tells us...

²² So Noah did everything exactly as God had commanded him.

Genesis 7:23-24, NLT is proof of God's promise which says

²³ God wiped out every living thing on the earth—people, livestock, small animals that scurry along the ground, and the birds of the sky. All were destroyed. The only people who survived were Noah and those with him in the boat.

²⁴ And the floodwaters covered the earth for 150 days.

God can rescue all believers when they trust and obey and apply James 1:19-25, NLT to their life it reads...

¹⁹ Understand this, my dear brothers and sisters: You must all be quick to listen, slow to speak, and slow to get angry.

²⁰ Human anger does not produce the righteousness God desires.

²¹ So get rid of all the filth and evil in your lives, and humbly accept the word God has planted in your hearts, for it has the power to save your souls.

²² But don't just listen to God's word. You must do what it says. Otherwise, you are only fooling yourselves.

²³ For if you listen to the word and don't obey, it is like glancing at your face in a mirror.

²⁴ You see yourself, walk away, and forget what you look like.

²⁵ But if you look carefully into the perfect law that sets you free, and if you do what it says and don't forget what you heard, then God will bless you for doing it.

God can bless you by stopping mental torment from troubling defeating thoughts.

God can bless you and give you emotional freedom from negative feelings.

God can bless you and keep your body healthy and free from sickness and disease.

The Holy Spirit can empower you to be joyful, content and satisfy.

The Holy Spirit can silence your mind and calm your heart issues. Your racing circling soulish thoughts will not dominate you as you dig deeper into the Word of God.

3 John 2, NKJV says:

[2] Beloved, I pray that you may prosper in all things and be in health, just as your soul prospers.

God wants all his sons and daughters to prosper. Once again as I have previously quoted, James 1:19-21, NLT says:

[19] Understand this, my dear brothers and sisters: You must all be quick to listen, slow to speak, and slow to get angry.

[20] Human anger does not produce the righteousness God desires.

[21] So get rid of all the filth and evil in your lives, and humbly accept the word God has planted in your hearts, for it has the power to save your souls.

To be quick to listen means a believer must be willing to listen to God's word instead of what the soulish natural thinks. Slow to speak means to listen instead of speaking your own ideas about right and wrong. Slow to become angry means a believer must not react against what God's word say and follow his or her own plan. Ephesians 4:26-27, NLT tells us...

[26] And "don't sin by letting anger control you." Don't let the sun go down while you are still angry,

[27] for anger gives a foothold to the devil.

Unresolved anger that turns into bitterness or resentment destroy your soul and body and weaken the immune system.

James 1:21-22, NLT reads: [21] So get rid of all the filth and evil in your lives, and humbly accept the word God has planted in your hearts, for it has the power to save your souls.

[22] But don't just listen to God's word. You must do what it says. Otherwise, you are only fooling yourselves.

As believers apply these verses, they will be blessed with mental health, emotional freedom, and deal less with physical illness. Stress hormones destroy the body when your soul is unhealthy.

The Greek word for filth (rup pair re a) is taken from the Greek word ruppus, which refers to wax in the ears.

Matthew 13:15, KJV speaks on a wax heart. It says...

[15] For this people's heart is waxed gross, and their ears are dull of hearing, and their eyes they have closed; lest at any time they should see with their eyes and hear with their ears, and should understand with their heart, and should be converted, and I should heal them.

God can heal a broken soul, painful soul, hurtful soul, crushed soul, or a grieving soul just by you making a decision to trust and obey his Word. Psalms 34:17-19, NLT, reads...

[17] The Lord hears his people when they call to him for help. He rescues them from all their troubles.

[18] The Lord is close to the brokenhearted; he rescues those whose spirits are crushed.

[19] The righteous person faces many troubles, but the Lord comes to the rescue each time.

Philippians 4:6-9, NLT, says...

[6] Don't worry about anything; instead, pray about every-thing. Tell God what you need, and thank him for all he has done.

⁷ Then you will experience God's peace, which exceeds anything we can understand. His peace will guard your hearts and minds as you live in Christ Jesus.

⁸ And now, dear brothers and sisters, one final thing. Fix your thoughts on what is true, and honorable, and right, and pure, and lovely, and admirable. Think about things that are excellent and worthy of praise.

⁹ Keep putting into practice all you learned and received from me—everything you heard from me and saw me doing. Then the God of peace will be with you.

God does not want any of his sons or daughters to be trouble in their soul. God wants his word printed on your heart.

Proverbs 3:1-8 NLT states...

¹My child, never forget the things I have taught you. Store my commands in your heart.
² If you do this, you will live many years, and your life will be satisfying.
³ Never let loyalty and kindness leave you! Tie them around your neck as a reminder. Write them deep within your heart.
⁴ Then you will find favor with both God and people, and you will earn a good reputation.
⁵ Trust in the Lord with all your heart; do not depend on your own understanding.
⁶ Seek his will in all you do, and he will show you which path to take.
⁷ Don't be impressed with your own wisdom. Instead, fear the Lord and turn away from evil.
⁸ Then you will have healing for your body and strength for your bones.

When you allow the fire of God burn in your heart and remain spiritual hot and not become lukewarm, your fire will never go out as you keep adding spiritual fuel, which is the Word of God. The last letter in Hot is T and stands for a teachable spirit.

When a believer has a Humble, Obedient, and Teachable spirit and is willing to turn from evil, he or she will hear the voice of God.

Proverbs 2:10-15, NLT says:

[10] For wisdom will enter your heart, and knowledge will fill you with joy.

[11] Wise choices will watch over you. Understanding will keep you safe.

[12] Wisdom will save you from evil people, from those whose words are twisted.

[13] These men turn from the right way to walk down dark paths.

[14] They take pleasure in doing wrong, and they enjoy the twisted ways of evil.

[15] Their actions are crooked, and their ways are wrong.

1 Peter 2:1-3, ESV

[1] So get rid of all evil behavior. Be done with all deceit, hypocrisy, jealousy, and all unkind speech.

[2] Like newborn babies, you must crave pure spiritual milk so that you will grow into a full experience of salvation. Cry out for this nourishment,

[3] now that you have had a taste of the Lord's kindness.

God wants people to grow up in their salvation and crave and desire His word by being humble and obedient.

Salvation is being delivered from sin and its consequences, and deliverance from harm, ruin or loss.

Jesus was an anointed, outstanding teacher who wants all believers to have a teachable spirit to hear His Word. Psalms 25:9, ESV explains:

[9] He leads the humble in what is right, and teaches the hum-

ble his way.

God wants his followers to grow up by implanting his Word in their heart to teach them to be mature.

Again in James 1:21-22, ESV it reads:

21 Therefore put away all filthiness and rampant wickedness and receive with meekness the implanted word, which is able to save your souls.

22 But be doers of the word, and not hearers only, deceiving yourselves.

God wants his sons and daughters to grow in grace and knowledge.

2 Peter 3:18, ESV says:

18 But grow in the grace and knowledge of our Lord and Savior Jesus Christ. To him be the glory both now and to the day of eternity. Amen.

Grace means favor and blessing from God and love and mercy he gives to all believers.

Growing in grace is to mature spiritually, but it is a continuing process.

God wants his sons and daughter's heart to have good soil that is soft and tender to receive spiritual nourishment to grow in knowledge. Proverbs 18:15, ESV and Proverbs 19:20, ESV reads:

15 Intelligent people are always ready to learn. Their ears are open for knowledge.

20 Get all the advice and instruction you can, so you will be wise the rest of your life.

Godly wisdom is the capability to make wise choices with no regrets.

We have to allow the anointing wise teacher Jesus to reshape us, mold us, and change us.

We are like an unpolished precious stone with many sharp and rough edges. God chips away at our character to reshape us into His image. He molds and shapes us until we can shine like a gem, he created us to be. As we meditate on the Word, we learn. Joshua 1:8-9, ESV can clarify it which says:

> [8] This Book of the Law shall not depart from your mouth, but you shall meditate on it day and night, so that you may be careful to do according to all that is written in it. For then you will make your way prosperous, and then you will have good success.

> [9] Have I not commanded you? Be strong and courageous. Do not be frightened, and do not be dismayed, for the Lord your God is with you wherever you go.

Proverbs 2:1-6, NLT states:

> [1] My child, listen to what I say, and treasure my commands.
> [2] Tune your ears to wisdom, and concentrate on understanding.
> [3] Cry out for insight, and ask for understanding.
> [4] Search for them as you would for silver; seek them like hidden treasures.
> [5] Then you will understand what it means to fear the Lord, and you will gain knowledge of God.
> [6] For the Lord grants wisdom! From his mouth come knowledge and understanding.

As we memorize scriptures, we grow to be like Jesus.

Psalms 119-7:15, ESV is a great example found in the Bible. It reads:

> [7] I will praise you with an upright heart, when I learn your righteous rules.
> [8] I will keep your statutes; do not utterly forsake me!

> [9] How can a young man keep his way pure? By guarding it according to your word.
> [10] With my whole heart I seek you; let me not wander from

your commandments!

¹¹ I have stored up your word in my heart, that I might not sin against you.

¹² Blessed are you, O Lord; teach me your statutes!

¹³ With my lips I declare all the rules of your mouth.

¹⁴ In the way of your testimonies I delight as much as in all riches.

¹⁵ I will meditate on your precepts and fix my eyes on your ways.

Luke 2:39-52, NLT is another example which reads:

³⁹ When Jesus' parents had fulfilled all the requirements of the law of the Lord, they returned home to Nazareth in Galilee.

⁴⁰ There the child grew up healthy and strong. He was filled with wisdom, and God's favor was on him.

⁴¹ Every year Jesus' parents went to Jerusalem for the Passover festival.

⁴² When Jesus was twelve years old, they attended the festival as usual.

⁴³ After the celebration was over, they started home to Nazareth, but Jesus stayed behind in Jerusalem. His parents didn't miss him at first,

⁴⁴ because they assumed he was among the other travelers. But when he didn't show up that evening, they started looking for him among their relatives and friends.

⁴⁵ When they couldn't find him, they went back to Jerusalem to search for him there.

⁴⁶ Three days later they finally discovered him in the Temple, sitting among the religious teachers, listening to them and asking questions.

⁴⁷ All who heard him were amazed at his understanding and his answers.

48 His parents didn't know what to think. "Son," his mother said to him, "why have you done this to us? Your father and I have been frantic, searching for you everywhere."

49 "But why did you need to search?" he asked. "Didn't you know that I must be in my Father's house?"

50 But they didn't understand what he meant.

51 Then he returned to Nazareth with them and was obedient to them. And his mother stored all these things in her heart.

52 Jesus grew in wisdom and in stature and in favor with God and all the people.

As we allow the Holy Spirit to mobilize us, we mature. James 1:22, ESV and Romans 8:5-9, ESV explains God's promises.

22 But be doers of the word, and not hearers only, deceiving yourselves.

5 For those who live according to the flesh set their minds on the things of the flesh, but those who live according to the Spirit set their minds on the things of the Spirit.

6 For to set the mind on the flesh is death, but to set the mind on the Spirit is life and peace.

7 For the mind that is set on the flesh is hostile to God, for it does not submit to God's law; indeed, it cannot.

8 Those who are in the flesh cannot please God.

9 You, however, are not in the flesh but in the Spirit, if in fact the Spirit of God dwells in you. Anyone who does not have the Spirit of Christ does not belong to him.

The Holy Spirit will teach you to trust and obey.

He will give you inner power to endure stressful times, devasting times, painful times, difficult times, and stormy times in life.

Isaiah 40:28-31, ESV tells us:

28 Have you not known? Have you not heard? The

Lord is the everlasting God, the Creator of the ends of the earth. He does not faint or grow weary; his understanding is unsearchable.

²⁹ He gives power to the faint, and to him who has no might he increases strength.

³⁰ Even youths shall faint and be weary, and young men shall fall exhausted;

³¹ but they who wait for the Lord shall renew their strength; they shall mount up with wings like eagles; they shall run and not be weary; they shall walk and not faint.

There may be lots of dark clouds in your life, but Jesus is the light of the world.

It may be thundering within your heart, but in times of difficult, stressful times, stormy times, he has super natural power to calm the storm in your heart.

The Holy Spirit helps his sons and daughters to dance in the pouring rain and nothing can steal our joy.

Our Heavenly Father is the only one that can make us whole in our soul to manage life here on earth successfully.

The winds of life will try to knock us down, but we know we are standing on holy ground.

The hard rough winds of life will only lead us above the clouds so we can soar higher.

God compares believers as eagles who can fly towards the storm as the storm approaches.

Eagles do not hide like other birds do. They fly into the aggressive winds and uses the storm current to rise higher.

The strong windy current pressure of the storm helps the eagle glide without using energy as their wings.

They choose to soar higher into Heaven which is the perfect place of peace and security.

As strong believers, we can use God's strength and God's

power to rise above the storms in life.

God's ways are higher and wiser. II Timothy 2:15, KJV says:

Study to shew thyself approved unto God, a workman that needeth not to be ashamed, rightly dividing the word of truth.

Psalms 32:8-11, NLT, says:

[8] The Lord says, "I will guide you along the best pathway for your life. I will advise you and watch over you.

[9] Do not be like a senseless horse or mule that needs a bit and bridle to keep it under control."

[10] Many sorrows come to the wicked, but unfailing love surrounds those who trust the Lord. [11] So rejoice in the Lord and be glad, all you who obey him!

Shout for joy, all you whose hearts are pure!

Remember to stay spiritually hot and on fire for Jesus. Keep your fire burning by letting the Word burn deep in your heart.

Having a Humble, Obedient and Teachable spirit will let you hear God speak to you.

So, I pray you find a quiet place every day to do a daily devotion or deep study on a topic of your interest to gain more knowledge and wisdom.

Some people in Israel disobeyed the Word of God and rejected the knowledge of God. Hosea 4:6, NKJV explains:

[6] My people are destroyed for lack of knowledge. Because you have rejected knowledge, I also will reject you from being priest for Me; Because you have forgotten the law of your God, I also will forget your children. My people are destroyed for lack of knowledge.

God does not want anyone to be destroyed. John 10:10, NKJV, says":

[10] The thief does not come except to steal, and to kill, and to destroy. I have come that they may have life, and that they

may have *it* more abundantly.

In order to live out the abundant, blessed, and joyful good life, believers must hear, listen, obey and apply the Word of God to their life.

Being blessed means having supernatural power working for us. The Holy Spirit gives us quality living here on earth. Mark 4:3-9, 18-19, NIV tells us:

³ "Listen! A farmer went out to sow his seed.

⁴ As he was scattering the seed, some fell along the path, and the birds came and ate it up.

⁵ Some fell on rocky places, where it did not have much soil. It sprang up quickly, because the soil was shallow.

⁶ But when the sun came up, the plants were scorched, and they withered because they had no root.

⁷ Other seed fell among thorns, which grew up and choked the plants, so that they did not bear grain.

⁸ Still other seed fell on good soil. It came up, grew and produced a crop, some multiplying thirty, some sixty, some a hundred times."

⁹ Then Jesus said, "Whoever has ears to hear, let them hear

¹⁸ Still others, like seed sown among thorns, hear the word;

¹⁹ but the worries of this life, the deceitfulness of wealth and the desires for other things come in and choke the word, making it unfruitful.

Grain symbolizes abundance, life, and fertility.

Spiritual fertility means to bring forth plentiful crops. God uses fertility as a metaphor to live out the fruitful life.

John 15:16, and Galatians 5:22-26, NLT says...

¹⁶ You didn't choose me. I chose you. I appointed you to go and produce lasting fruit, so that the Father will give you whatever you ask for, using my name.

²² But the Holy Spirit produces this kind of fruit in our lives: love, joy, peace, patience, kindness, goodness, faithfulness,

²³ gentleness, and self-control. There is no law against these things!

²⁴ Those who belong to Christ Jesus have nailed the passions and desires of their sinful nature to his cross and crucified them there.

²⁵ Since we are living by the Spirit, let us follow the Spirit's leading in every part of our lives.

²⁶ Let us not become conceited, or provoke one another, or be jealous of one another.

The next seed fell among thorns. It is hard to produce crops with a **thorny heart soil** which permits little root to go into it. This person allowed the thorns to choke the plant (Word) and strangled life out of him or her with a trouble worried mindset. God is the only one that can give a believer a peace of mind if you give Him some time.

I am sure you all heard "you are going to worry yourself to death." Worrying only affects your daily life. It interferes with focusing and being productive.

As believers, seek God, trust God, and have faith in God all the stresses, worries, demands, and pressures will be more manageable. Worrying will not control or dominate and drain your brain and emotional energy.

The outpouring of stress hormones in the blood for a long period can cause minor damage to severe in the body such as:

- Headaches
- Stomach issues
- Nausea
- Nervous energy
- High blood pressure

- Ulcers
- Week immune system
- Heart attack
- Short memory loss

Just to mention some effects of worrying. Matthew 6:25-27, 31:34, NIV, says:

> **25** "Therefore I tell you, do not worry about your life, what you will eat or drink; or about your body, what you will wear. Is not life more than food, and the body more than clothes?
>
> **26** Look at the birds of the air; they do not sow or reap or store away in barns, and yet your heavenly Father feeds them. Are you not much more valuable than they?
>
> **27** Can any one of you by worrying add a single hour to your life?
>
> **31** So do not worry, saying, 'What shall we eat?' or 'What shall we drink?' or 'What shall we wear?'
>
> **32** For the pagans run after all these things, and your heavenly Father knows that you need them.
>
> **33** But seek first his kingdom and his righteousness, and all these things will be given to you as well.
>
> **34** Therefore do not worry about tomorrow, for tomorrow will worry about itself. Each day has enough trouble of its own.

The devil's evil plan is to use fear, anxiety or worry to control a person and overwhelm him or her. The four paws of satan are to destroy your soul and body.

The P in Paws stands for Panic Attitude. This person has lack of confidence and no strength within. The trials of life left this person fearful and him or her is barely functioning.

God's Word propels you to choose faith over fear. Read the three scriptures below and let them penetrate your heart. II Timothy 1:7, NJKV says:

> [7] For God has not given us a spirit of fear, but of power and of love and of a sound mind.

Isaiah 41:10, NLT, reads…

> [10] Don't be afraid, for I am with you. Don't be discouraged, for I am your God. I will strengthen you and help you. I will hold you up with my victorious right hand.

Psalms 94:19, NIV, says…

> [19] When anxiety was great within me, your consolation brought me joy.

There is no need to fear, God is nearby. Fear is:

> False
>
> Evidence
>
> Appearing
>
> Real

There is godly fear which means a sense of respect and to hate evil, pride, and arrogance.

Proverbs 8:13, 10:27, and 15:33, NLT, reads..

> [13] All who fear the Lord will hate evil. Therefore, I hate pride and arrogance, corruption and perverse speech.

> [27] Fear of the Lord lengthens one's life, but the years of the wicked are cut short.

> [33] Fear of the Lord teaches wisdom; humility precedes honor.

The second letter in Paws is A which stands for an Anxious Attitude.

This person worries excessively and has lost his or her sense of security.This person thoughts are always on "what if?", "what if this happens?", or "what if that occurs?". Excessive worrying can interface with daily life.

It is natural to be concerned, but God does not want his sons and daughters to worry themselves to death. The devil tries to use worry to make one weak. The Holy Spirit replaces worry with peace when you trust Him.

Here are three great scriptures to remember when having worried thoughts. Proverbs 12:25, NLT, tells us:

²⁵ Worry weighs a person down; an encouraging word cheers a person up.

1 Peter 5:7, NLT reads:

⁷ Give all your worries and cares to God, for he cares about you.

God wants all believers to stand firm with the signs of ends times. He told us believers would be persecuted close to end times.

Luke 21:9-19, NIV, states:

⁹ When you hear of wars and uprisings, do not be frightened. These things must happen first, but the end will not come right away."

¹⁰ Then he said to them: "Nation will rise against nation, and kingdom against kingdom.

¹¹ There will be great earthquakes, famines and pestilences in various places, and fearful events and great signs from heaven.

¹² "But before all this, they will seize you and persecute you. They will hand you over to synagogues and put you in prison, and you will be brought before kings and governors, and all on account of my name.

¹³ And so you will bear testimony to me.

¹⁴ But make up your mind not to worry beforehand how you will defend yourselves.

¹⁵ For I will give you words and wisdom that none of your

adversaries will be able to resist or contradict.

[16] You will be betrayed even by parents, brothers and sisters, relatives and friends, and they will put some of you to death.

[17] Everyone will hate you because of me.

[18] But not a hair of your head will perish.

[19] Stand firm, and you will win life.

The third letter in Paws stands for Worldly Attitude. This person has very little concern about the future. Earthly pleasure consumes the person's soul on what they do not have. The ruler of darkness tries to get a person to cave in and give into buying material things to suck life out of the person. Materialism can drown your energy and put someone in a stressful worried mindset trying to keep up with the Jones'.

These three scriptures will explain: Proverbs 14:30, NIV says:

[30] A heart at peace gives life to the body, but envy rots the bones.

The heart at peace is blessed with emotional health while the person who has envy in his or her heart is like cancer eating at their bones.

Mark 7:18-23, NLT reads:

[18] "Don't you understand either?" he asked. "Can't you see that the food you put into your body cannot defile you?

[19] Food doesn't go into your heart, but only passes through the stomach and then goes into the sewer." (By saying this, he declared that every kind of food is acceptable in God's eyes.)

[20] And then he added, "It is what comes from inside that defiles you.

[21] For from within, out of a person's heart, come evil

thoughts, sexual immorality, theft, murder,

²² adultery, greed, wickedness, deceit, lustful desires, envy, slander, pride, and foolishness.

²³ All these vile things come from within; they are what defile you."

God does not want any believer to be contaminated by this evil fallen world. James 3:13-16, NLT tells us:

¹³ If you are wise and understand God's ways, prove it by living an honorable life, doing good works with the humility that comes from wisdom.

¹⁴ But if you are bitterly jealous and there is selfish ambition in your heart, don't cover up the truth with boasting and lying.

¹⁵ For jealousy and selfishness are not God's kind of wisdom. Such things are earthly, unspiritual, and demonic.

¹⁶ For wherever there is jealousy and selfish ambition, there you will find disorder and evil of every kind.

The last letter in Paws is S and that stands for Self Sufficient Attitude. This person does not have godly confidence or godly ability. This person only relies on self-confidence and self-ability and misses out on what God can do. The person leaves God out of the equation and takes pride in his or her accomplishments.

Let these three scriptures go deep in your heart.

Jeremiah 17:7, NLT

⁷ "But blessed are those who trust in the Lord and have made the Lord their hope and confidence.

2 Corinthians 3:3-5, ESV

³ And you show that you are a letter from Christ delivered

by us, written not with ink but with the Spirit of the living God, not on tablets of stone but on tablets of human hearts. [4] Such is the confidence that we have through Christ toward God.

[5] Not that we are sufficient in ourselves to claim anything as coming from us, but our sufficiency is from God,

2 Corinthians 12:7-10, ESV

[7] So to keep me from becoming conceited because of the surpassing greatness of the revelations, a thorn was given me in the flesh, a messenger of Satan to harass me, to keep me from becoming conceited.

[8] Three times I pleaded with the Lord about this, that it should leave me.

[9] But he said to me, "My grace is sufficient for you, for my power is made perfect in weakness." Therefore I will boast all the more gladly of my weaknesses, so that the power of Christ may rest upon me.

[10] For the sake of Christ, then, I am content with weaknesses, insults, hardships, persecutions, and calamities. For when I am weak, then I am strong.

As sons and daughters with a trusting attitude of godly confidence, God can take care of all your worries.

Proverbs 3:5-6, NKJV, reads…

[5] Trust in the Lord with all your heart, And lean not on your own understanding;
[6] In all your ways acknowledge Him, And He shall direct your paths.

The Bible give all believers coping strategies so the thorns in life is less hurtful and painful. As a believer researches scripture, the Holy Spirit will bless every one of his sons and daughters with health soul and body.

The Holy Spirit will prevent mental confusion, emotional

exhaustion, physical fatigue, and spiritual burnout. You will not be strangled by the thorns in life as you dig deeper into the Word of God. Nothing can steal your peace of mind with worried thoughts any more.

Mark 4:1-9, NLT, reads...

[1]Once again Jesus began teaching by the lakeshore. A very large crowd soon gathered around him, so he got into a boat. Then he sat in the boat while all the people remained on the shore.

[2] He taught them by telling many stories in the form of parables, such as this one:

[3] "Listen! A farmer went out to plant some seed.

[4] As he scattered it across his field, some of the seed fell on a footpath, and the birds came and ate it.

[5] Other seed fell on shallow soil with underlying rock. The seed sprouted quickly because the soil was shallow.

[6] But the plant soon wilted under the hot sun, and since it didn't have deep roots, it died.

[7] Other seed fell among thorns that grew up and choked out the tender plants so they produced no grain.

[8] Still other seeds fell on fertile soil, and they sprouted, grew, and produced a crop that was thirty, sixty, and even a hundred times as much as had been planted!"

[9] Then he said, "Anyone with ears to hear should listen and understand."

The **good-hearted soil** is the last ground the seed fell on, but it had strong, deep roots. It produced a fruitful life.

This believer is growing in godly knowledge and applying wisdom. The word of God will bless his sons and daughters with peace of mind and a calm heart because it produced crops.

So, the second and third types of soil (heart) were not working with the seed (Word). All three seeds could not get strong deep roots because the person's soul was troubled.

The <u>hard</u>-hearted heart had no roots which can lead to having an empty heart due to the wandering mindset. The devil stole the Word.

The <u>rocky</u> heart had some roots and was blessed hearing the Word. This believer got encouraged by God's promises. As soon as problems, issues, or trouble came, they became confused. The roots needed more nourishment but the hot sun took the Word away.

The <u>thorny</u> heart had little roots, but got distracted by the worries in life. This believer was restless with a worried mindset. The thorns of life strangled the Word out of his or her life.

God can take a believer's hard-hearted heart, rocky heart, or thorny heart and give the believer a good heart with rich fertilizer.

Ezekiel 36:26, Common English Bible (CEB) tell us "I will give you a new heart and put a new spirit in you. I will remove the stony heart from your body and replace it with a living one." Jesus is the living stone and He calls believers living stones also. It tells us this in 1 Peter 2:4-5 NIV:

As you come to him, the living Stone—rejected by humans but chosen by God and precious to him— 5 you also, like living stones, are being built into a spiritual house[a] to be a holy priesthood, offering spiritual sacrifices acceptable to God through Jesus Christ.

In order for a plant to grow, it is essential to keep the PH between 6.5 to 7. A PH low stunts roots and a PH too high stunts roots.

God is our PH and he wants his sons and daughters to grow and be a developed and be a strong Christian and victorious believer. God is the physician healer. In Matthew 9:9-12, ESV it reads:

⁹ As Jesus passed on from there, he saw a man called Matthew sitting at the tax booth, and he said to him, "Follow me." And he rose and followed him.

¹⁰ And as Jesus reclined at table in the house, behold, many tax collectors and sinners came and were reclining with Jesus and his disciples.

¹¹ And when the Pharisees saw this, they said to his disciples, "Why does your teacher eat with tax collectors and sinners?"

¹² But when he heard it, he said, "Those who are well have no need of a physician, but those who are sick.

The Holy Spirit wants believers to receive and have the Word of God deeply rooted in their hearts to heal the sick soul and body. Ezekiel 2:1-3, 3:7-11 and 8:9 ESV, it states:

¹And he said to me, "Son of man, stand on your feet, and I will speak with you."

² And as he spoke to me, the Spirit entered into me and set me on my feet, and I heard him speaking to me.

³ And he said to me, "Son of man, I send you to the people of Israel, to nations of rebels, who have rebelled against me. They and their fathers have transgressed against me to this very day.

Ezekiel 3:7-11 But the house of Israel will not be willing to listen to you, for they are not willing to listen to me: because all the house of Israel have a hard forehead and a stubborn heart.

⁸ Behold, I have made your face as hard as their faces, and your forehead as hard as their foreheads.

⁹ Like emery harder than flint have I made your forehead. Fear them not, nor be dismayed at their looks, for they are a rebellious house."

¹⁰ Moreover, he said to me, "Son of man, all my words that I

shall speak to you receive in your heart, and hear with your ears.

¹¹ And go to the exiles, to your people, and speak to them and say to them, 'Thus says the Lord God,' whether they hear or refuse to hear

Ezekiel 8:9 And he said to me, "Go in, and see the vile abominations that they are committing here.

Flint means back lines running through the bones colored rock. If flint is hit with steel, it sparks. Sparks are like neutrons in the brain which are chemical messengers that transmit messages between neurons to communicate.

According in Matthew Henry's concise commentary, the true context means "Ezekiel was to receive the truths of God as the food for his soul, and the feed upon them by faith and he would be strengthened. Gracious souls can receive those truths of God with delight, which speak terror to the wicked"

God knows how wicked and sick the heart is. He wants the Word to give you a good heart. He was the one who made your heart. Jeremiah 17:5-9, NLT, explains and tell us:

⁵ This is what the Lord says: "Cursed are those who put their trust in mere humans, who rely on human strength and turn their hearts away from the Lord.
⁶ They are like stunted shrubs in the desert, with no hope for the future. They will live in the barren wilderness, in an uninhabited salty land.

⁷ "But blessed are those who trust in the Lord and have made the Lord their hope and confidence.
⁸ They are like trees planted along a riverbank, with roots that reach deep into the water. Such trees are not bothered by the eat or worried by long months of drought. Their leaves stay green, and they never stop producing fruit.

[9] "The human heart is the most deceitful of all things, and desperately wicked. Who really knows how bad it is?

God knows the secrets of everyone hearts and he is a merciful God. God can take the veil over your heart and remove the unclean spirits that only torment your soul if you have a conscience between right and wrong. 2 Corinthians 3:9-18, NLT, reads:

[9] If the old way, which brings condemnation, was glorious, how much more glorious is the new way, which makes us right with God!

[10] In fact, that first glory was not glorious at all compared with the overwhelming glory of the new way.

[11] So if the old way, which has been replaced, was glorious, how much more glorious is the new, which remains forever!

[12] Since this new way gives us such confidence, we can be very bold.

[13] We are not like Moses, who put a veil over his face so the people of Israel would not see the glory, even though it was destined to fade away.

[14] But the people's minds were hardened, and to this day whenever the old covenant is being read, the same veil covers their minds so they cannot understand the truth. And this veil can be removed only by believing in Christ.

[15] Yes, even today when they read Moses' writings, their hearts are covered with that veil, and they do not understand.

[16] But whenever someone turns to the Lord, the veil is taken away.

[17] For the Lord is the Spirit, and wherever the Spirit of the Lord is, there is freedom.

[18] So all of us who have had that veil removed can see and reflect the glory of the Lord. And the Lord—who is the Spirit

—makes us more and more like him as we are changed into his glorious image.

Moses spent a lot of time with God. People saw God's glory on Moses' face. God has the power to give all believers emotional freedom. Our Heavenly Father can cleanse his sons and daughters from anger, bitterness, fear, guilt, hate, and unforgiveness. This way the Word of God can penetrate deep within their heart with the right good soil. In Chapter 3, I will explain on emotional freedom.

Hebrews 4:12-13, NLT, reads…

¹² For the word of God is alive and powerful. It is sharper than the sharpest two-edged sword, cutting between soul and spirit, between joint and marrow. It exposes our innermost thoughts and desires.

¹³ Nothing in all creation is hidden from God. Everything is naked and exposed before his eyes, and he is the one to whom we are accountable.

Let me explain the Words living, active, sharper and penetrating. The Word of God is "living reality, it is full of life to the heart of the believer. The Word will always give you an uplifting message.

The Word of God is active. It energizes the heart of the believer and causes all believers to rest in God's presence. It is true place within good times and bad.

The Word of God is sharper than any double-edged sword. It uncovers the unresolved emotional issues and gives the soul rest.

The Word of God penetrates the heart. It goes right to the soul and spirit of a believer. It separates the soulish nature from divine spirit being.

It separates an unbelieving soul from a believing spirit.

It separates a proud soul from a humble spirit.

It separates a rebellious soul from an obedient spirit.

The Word of God analyzes the thoughts and the intents of the believer's heart. Ecclesiastes 12:13-14, NLT, states:

> [13] That's the whole story. Here now is my final conclusion: Fear God and obey his commands, for this is everyone's duty.
>
> [14] God will judge us for everything we do, including every secret thing, whether good or bad.

God is a righteous judge. He must act justly and judge to save us from his wrath. Romans 5:3-9, NLT, reads…

> [3] We can rejoice, too, when we run into problems and trials, for we know that they help us develop endurance.
>
> [4] And endurance develops strength of character, and character strengthens our confident hope of salvation.
>
> [5] And this hope will not lead to disappointment. For we know how dearly God loves us, because he has given us the Holy Spirit to fill our hearts with his love.
>
> [6] When we were utterly helpless, Christ came at just the right time and died for us sinners.
>
> [7] Now, most people would not be willing to die for an upright person, though someone might perhaps be willing to die for a person who is especially good.
>
> [8] But God showed his great love for us by sending Christ to die for us while we were still sinners.
>
> [9] And since we have been made right in God's sight by the blood of Christ, he will certainly save us from God's condemnation.

The Word of God only lifts us up and builds us up. Acts 20:32, NLT, says…

³² "And now I entrust you to God and the message of his grace that is able to build you up and give you an inheritance with all those he has set apart for himself.

Ephesians 1:11-14, ESV tells us one of a believer's inheritance is the Holy Spirit, which reads...

¹¹ In him we have obtained an inheritance, having been predestined according to the purpose of him who works all things according to the counsel of his will,

¹² so that we who were the first to hope in Christ might be to the praise of his glory.

¹³ In him you also, when you heard the word of truth, the gospel of your salvation, and believed in him, were sealed with the promised Holy Spirit,

¹⁴ who is the guarantee of our inheritance until we acquire possession of it, to the praise of his glory.

This seal is a guarantee we belong to God and shows ownership. It provides us with protection and security.

God protected the:

- Three Hebrew men who got saved from the fiery furnace
- Daniel got rescued from the lions' den
- God used Ruth to save the Jews from all being killed
- God saved Noah and his family from the flood
- God saved the adultery woman from being stoned to death
- God saved the Israelites across the Red Sea unharmed
- God rescued Job from satan's evil plan

In Job 1:1-3, 8-19 Job lost his herd. In the NLT, It reads:

1 There once was a man named Job who lived in the land of Uz. He was blameless—a man of complete integrity. He feared God and stayed away from evil.

² He had seven sons and three daughters.

³ He owned 7,000 sheep, 3,000 camels, 500 teams of oxen, and 500 female donkeys. He also had many servants. He was, in fact, the richest person in that entire area.

⁸ Then the Lord asked Satan, "Have you noticed my servant Job? He is the finest man in all the earth. He is blameless— a man of complete integrity. He fears God and stays away from evil."

⁹ Satan replied to the Lord, "Yes, but Job has good reason to fear God.

¹⁰ You have always put a wall of protection around him and his home and his property. You have made him prosper in everything he does. Look how rich he is!

¹¹ But reach out and take away everything he has, and he will surely curse you to your face!"

¹² "All right, you may test him," the Lord said to Satan. "Do whatever you want with everything he possesses, but don't harm him physically." So Satan left the Lord's presence.

13 One day when Job's sons and daughters were feasting at the oldest brother's house, 14 a messenger arrived at Job's home with this news: "Your oxen were plowing, with the donkeys feeding beside them, 15 when the Sabeans raided us. They stole all the animals and killed all the farmhands. I am the only one who escaped to tell you."

16 While he was still speaking, another messenger arrived with this news: "The fire of God has fallen from heaven and burned up your sheep and all the shepherds. I am the only one who escaped to tell you."

17 While he was still speaking, a third messenger arrived with this news: "Three bands of Chaldean raiders have stolen your camels and killed your servants. I am the only

one who escaped to tell you."

18 While he was still speaking, another messenger arrived with this news: "Your sons and daughters were feasting in their oldest brother's home. 19 Suddenly, a powerful wind swept in from the wilderness and hit the house on all sides. The house collapsed, and all your children are dead. I am the only one who escaped to tell you."

Now, read Job's response in Job 1:20-22, NLT which states :

20 Job stood up and tore his robe in grief. Then he shaved his head and fell to the ground to worship.

21 He said, "I came naked from my mother's womb, and I will be naked when I leave. The Lord gave me what I had, and the Lord has taken it away. Praise the name of the Lord!"

22 In all of this, Job did not sin by blaming God.

Job's second test can be found in Job 2: 4-10 NLT which reads:

4 Satan replied to the Lord, "Skin for skin! A man will give up everything he has to save his life. 5 But reach out and take away his health, and he will surely curse you to your face!"

6 "All right, do with him as you please," the Lord said to Satan. "But spare his life." 7 So Satan left the Lord's presence, and he struck Job with terrible boils from head to foot.

8 Job scraped his skin with a piece of broken pottery as he sat among the ashes. 9 His wife said to him, "Are you still trying to maintain your integrity? Curse God and die."

10 But Job replied, "You talk like a foolish woman. Should we accept only good things from the hand of God and never anything bad?" So in all this, Job said nothing wrong. Because David trusted God, he killed the big giant Goliath.

Job was a righteous man with a pure heart. God blessed Job back and restored everything back with extra blessing.

In Job 42:12-13, NLT it tells us:

12 So the Lord blessed Job in the second half of his life even more than in the beginning. For now he had 14,000 sheep, 6,000 camels, 1,000 teams of oxen, and 1,000 female donkeys. 13 He also gave Job seven more sons and three more daughters. 14 He named his first daughter Jemimah, the second Keziah, and the third Keren-happuch.

God will always rescue all believers and give them victory. God gave David victory.

1 Samuel 17:45-51, NLT, states...

45 David replied to the Philistine, "You come to me with sword, spear, and javelin, but I come to you in the name of the Lord of Heaven's Armies—the God of the armies of Israel, whom you have defied.

46 Today the Lord will conquer you, and I will kill you and cut off your head. And then I will give the dead bodies of your men to the birds and wild animals, and the whole world will know that there is a God in Israel!

47 And everyone assembled here will know that the Lord rescues his people, but not with sword and spear. This is the Lord's battle, and he will give you to us!"

48 As Goliath moved closer to attack, David quickly ran out to meet him.

49 Reaching into his shepherd's bag and taking out a stone, he hurled it with his sling and hit the Philistine in the forehead. The stone sank in, and Goliath stumbled and fell face down on the ground.

50 So David triumphed over the Philistine with only a sling and a stone, for he had no sword.

51 Then David ran over and pulled Goliath's sword from its sheath. David used it to kill him and cut off his head.

It is victory when you trust God. God restored everything back to Job when he trusted Him.

Lastly 2 Peter 2:9 states:

9then the Lord knows how to rescue the godly from trials, [a] and to keep the unrighteous under punishment until the day of judgment,

CHAPTER 2 PUT ON THE ATTITUDE OF JESUS

The Bible states in Philippians 2:5-11, NLT:

[5] You must have the same attitude that Christ Jesus had.

[6] Though he was God, he did not think of equality with God as something to cling to.

[7] Instead, he gave up his divine privileges he took the humble position of a slave and was born as a human being. When he appeared in human form,

[8] he humbled himself in obedience to God and died a criminal's death on a cross. Therefore, God elevated him to the place of highest honor and gave him the name above all other names,

[10] that at the name of Jesus every knee should bow, in heaven and on earth and under the earth,

[11] and every tongue declare that Jesus Christ is Lord, to the glory of God the Father.

God wants all believers to have a humble attitude. Believers should recognize God's help, knowing our strength is limited and His supernatural strength is unlimited.

Philippians 4:13, NKJV tells us:

[13] I can do all things through Christ who strengthens me.

Having the attitude of Jesus and working together in unity we can help unbelievers and baby Christians be blessed with a sense of security and peace of mind.

Philippians 2:3-4, NLT:

³ Don't be selfish; don't try to impress others. Be humble, thinking of others as better than yourselves. ⁴ Don't look out only for your own interests, but take an interest in others, too.

God's Word says to bear one another's burdens, when a believer is struggling with a difficult situation. In Galatians 6:2-3 NLT reads:

² Share each other's burdens, and in this way obey the law of Christ. ³ If you think you are too important to help someone, you are only fooling yourself. You are not that important.

Taking care of unbelievers and new baby Christians is the responsibility of all believers, to lead him or her to have the attitude of Jesus and give them victory over mental stress.

Unhealthy thoughts that can cause a great deal of emotional distress. When you find yourself thinking in unhealthy ways such as:

- Dwelling on the negative

- Believing the worst outcome

- Disqualifying the positive

- Jumping to conclusions

- Maximizing the problem

- Minimizing the issue

- Personalizing everything

- Emotional reasoning which overrules rational thoughts.

Rational spiritual thinking will heal your soul faster than your selfish being. The Bible provides practical wisdom to help us manage mental stress successfully.

It is crucial to realize that your own natural thinking is completely different from God's way of thinking. Isaiah 55:8-9, NIV explains:

> 8 "For my thoughts are not your thoughts, neither are your ways my ways,"
> declares the Lord.
>
> 9 "As the heavens are higher than the earth, so are my ways higher than your ways
> and my thoughts than your thoughts.

God even tells us how to think and take care of our soul, which is the mind, emotions, and will. Philippians 4:6-9, NLT:

> 6 Don't worry about anything; instead, pray about everything. Tell God what you need, and thank him for all he has done. 7 Then you will experience God's peace, which exceeds anything we can understand. His peace will guard your hearts and minds as you live in Christ Jesus.
> 8 And now, dear brothers and sisters, one final thing. Fix your thoughts on what is true, and honorable, and right, and pure, and lovely, and admirable. Think about things that are excellent and worthy of praise. 9 Keep putting into practice all you learned and received from me—everything you heard from me and saw me doing. Then the God of peace will be with you.

The word *mind* is translated from Hebrew as *reins*. Reins lead, control, and direct. Our mind is just like reins which guide our emotional life. God wants us to yield to the Holy Spirit so we can have a happy, cheerful soul. David in the Bible had victory. Psalm 32:7-9, NLT reads:

> 7 For you are my hiding place; you protect me from trouble. You surround me with songs of victory. *Interlude*
> 8 The Lord says, "I will guide you along the best pathway for your life. I will advise you and watch over you.
> 9 Do not be like a senseless horse or mule that needs a bit and bridle to keep it under control."

As Christians we should not depend on our way of thinking.

In Proverbs 3:5-6, NIV is a great scripture to store in our long-term memory, to quote when in need. It states:

> [5] Trust in the Lord with all your heart and lean not on your own understanding;
>
> [6] in all your ways submit to him, and he will make your paths straight.

By training our mind to think like Jesus, we will be victorious no matter what we go through in life. God tells us that storms often come from the south. The word *south* in the Hebrew is *chedar*, which describes the innermost part of our mind. Job 37:9 in the New American Standard Bible reads:

> "Out of the south comes the storm, And out of the north the cold.

As we allow the word of God to go down into the innermost part of our subconscious, we begin to change and truly experience the peace of God. Isaiah 26:3-4, in the Easy-To- Read Version:

> [3] God, you give true peace to people who depend on you,
>   to those who trust in you.
> [4] So trust the Lord always, because in the Lord Yah you have a place of safety forever.

When we allow the Holy Spirit to transform our carnal mind into a spiritual mind, we are blessed. Romans 8:6-8, NIV:

> [6] The mind governed by the flesh is death, but the mind governed by the Spirit is life and peace. [7] The mind governed by the flesh is hostile to God; it does not submit to God's law, nor can it do so. [8] Those who are in the realm of the flesh cannot please God.

It is a believer's responsibility to renew his or her mind every day, to have the attitude of Jesus. The scripture Romans 12:2, says in the NIV:

> [2] Do not conform to the pattern of this world, but be

transformed by the renewing of your mind. Then you will be able to test and approve what God's will is—his good, pleasing and perfect will.

It is also a believer's responsibility to take captive every thought that does not line up with the Word of God. In the 2 Corinthians 10:4-5, NKJV it states:

> 4 For the weapons of our warfare *are* not carnal but mighty in God for pulling down strongholds,

> 5 casting down arguments and every high thing that exalts itself against the knowledge of God, bringing every thought into captivity to the obedience of Christ...

The Greek word for strongholds means fortress, which is representative of thoughts. Strongholds are thoughts which damage our soul and body and go against the knowledge and wisdom of God. These include:

- Human philosophy
- False theory
- Worldly outlook
- A lack of faith
- Prideful attitude
- Obsessive thoughts to overcome and addiction
- Distorted perceptions
- Lies from the devil that lead to false belief.

The devil is the enemy of your soul, but God blesses all believers with mental and emotional freedom. He will empower you to live in freedom and give you peace of mind.

God wants all believers' souls to prosper. In 3 John, verse 2, NKJV, it reads:

> 2 Beloved, I pray that you may prosper in all things and be in health, just as your soul prospers.

You may think, how can my soul prosper and gain the victory over the stressors in life? Here is the solution: think of these three words that start with the letter M:

- Meditate

- Memorize

- Mobilize

When we do all three, we learn, grow, and mature into God's image.

Joshua 1:8, NIV, tells us to <u>meditate</u> on God's promises. Let this scripture sink into your heart:

> [8] Keep this Book of the Law always on your lips; meditate on it day and night, so that you may be careful to do everything written in it. Then you will be prosperous and successful.

Psalms 119:11, NIV tells us to memorize the scriptures:

> [11] I have hidden your word in my heart that I might not sin against you.

Do you have scriptures in your heart to say to yourself, to encourage yourself, to stay focused and move forward when going through tough times?

Are you a doer of God's promises? James 1:22, ESV tells us to mobilize the Word:

> [22] But be doers of the word, and not hearers only, deceiving yourselves.

The Holy Spirit helped me apply His word to a very stressful situation when I co-signed for a car for my husband when we were separated. Wells Fargo Bank was taking $100.00 a week out of my paycheck to pay off a $10,000 loan. I was very angry and discouraged. I wanted answers and I wanted my peace of mind back. So, I started to read Proverbs and came across Proverbs 11:15, God's Word Translation:

> [15] Whoever guarantees a stranger's loan will get into trouble, but whoever hates the closing of a deal remains

secure.

I got my peace of mind back when I paid it off in full. The Bible has solutions for everything we face on earth. Now, of course my husband was not a stranger but only God knows the true heart of a person because my husband's heart was with another woman.

So, remember meditating, memorizing, and mobilizing. the Word of God is where we learn to manage the pressures and problems in life. He gives us peace in the midst of the storms in life. Isaiah 9:6 tells us Jesus is the Prince of Peace. Listen to these two scriptures.

John 14:27, NLT:

27 "I am leaving you with a gift—peace of mind and heart. And the peace I give is a gift the world cannot give. So don't be troubled or afraid.

Isaiah 26:3-4, NLT:

You will keep in perfect peace all who trust in you, all whose thoughts are fixed on you!

4 Trust in the Lord always, for the Lord God is the eternal Rock.

As Christians we can win this spiritual warfare and every mental battle. God makes us a strong Christian soldier when we keep the whole armor on. Ephesians 6:11-18, TLB:

11 Put on all of God's armor so that you will be able to stand safe against all strategies and tricks of Satan.

12 For we are not fighting against people made of flesh and blood, but against persons without bodies—the evil rulers of the unseen world, those mighty satanic beings and great evil princes of darkness who rule this world; and against huge numbers of wicked spirits in the spirit world.

13 So use every piece of God's armor to resist the enemy whenever he attacks, and when it is all over, you will still be standing up.

¹⁴ But to do this, you will need the strong belt of truth and the breastplate of God's approval.

¹⁵ Wear shoes that are able to speed you on as you preach the Good News of peace with God.

¹⁶ In every battle you will need faith as your shield to stop the fiery arrows aimed at you by Satan.

¹⁷ And you will need the helmet of salvation and the sword of the Spirit—which is the Word of God.

¹⁸ Pray all the time. Ask God for anything in line with the Holy Spirit's wishes. Plead with him, reminding him of your needs, and keep praying earnestly for all Christians everywhere.

The helmet of salvation protects our spiritual mind. The Roman soldiers used it to protect their heads from injury. In a spiritual perspective, the helmet protects the center of our thoughts. Salvation delivers us from believing and embracing lies, because the Holy Spirit reveals the truth to our minds. The devil tries to attack believers with a powerful blow of doubt into our mind. Satan's main goal is for a believer not to trust God and turn us away from God. Listen to what 2 Timothy 2:3-4 tells us in the NIV:

³ Join with me in suffering, like a good soldier of Christ Jesus.

⁴ No one serving as a soldier gets entangled in civilian affairs, but rather tries to please his commanding officer.

Strong Christian soldiers are not distracted by civilian concerns. A Christian's main focus is to follow instruction from his or her anointed Pastor who leads them. Hebrews 13:17, NLT reads:

¹⁷ Obey your spiritual leaders, and do what they say. Their work is to watch over your souls, and they are accountable to God. Give them reason to do this with joy and not with sorrow. That would certainly not be for your benefit.

God wants our minds to be sharp and alert to boost our mental performance.Together we can achieve, believe, and receive by keeping a righteous attitude like Jesus. God wants us to stop overthinking and trust Him.

One thing about mental health – we must be aware of our overthinking mindset that causes a great amount of emotional stress. God tells us, in Philippians 4:6-7, NKJV, which is different words from the NLT:

> [6] Be anxious for nothing, but in everything by prayer and supplication, with thanksgiving, let your requests be made known to God;
>
> [7] and the peace of God, which surpasses all understanding, will guard your hearts and minds through Christ Jesus.

1 Peter 5:6-11 NKJV tells us to:

> [6] Humble yourselves, therefore, under God's mighty hand, that he may lift you up in due time.
> [7] cast[ing] all your care upon Him, for He cares for you.
> [8] Be sober, be vigilant; because your adversary the devil walks about like a roaring lion, seeking whom he may devour.
> [9] Resist him, steadfast in the faith, knowing that the same sufferings are experienced by your brotherhood in the world.
> [10] But may the God of all grace, who called us to His eternal glory by Christ Jesus, after you have suffered a while, perfect, establish, strengthen, and settle *you.*
> [11] To Him *be* the glory and the dominion forever and ever. Amen.

This is how a person knows if they are under mental fatigue. Think using the acronym "DOT OF" to remember:

- Difficulty Making Decisions

- Obsessive Thoughts

- Trouble Concentrating

. Overthinking

• Forgetfulness

God is not the author of confusion, it tells us in 1 Corinthians 14:33, NKJV.

³³ For God is not *the author* of confusion but of peace, as in all the churches of the saints.

The devil's goal is to prevent unbelievers from knowing the truth so they will not be saved. In John 14:6, NKJV, it states:

⁶ Jesus said to him, "I am the way, the truth, and the life. No one comes to the Father except through Me.

Satan wants to keep unbelievers blind but the Supernatural Power of God can open the eyes of the blind. The Bible says in 2 Corinthians 4:3-10, NLT and Psalm 146:8, in the NLT:

³ If the Good News we preach is hidden behind a veil, it is hidden only from people who are perishing.
⁴ Satan, who is the god of this world, has blinded the minds of those who don't believe. They are unable to see the glorious light of the Good News. They don't understand this message about the glory of Christ, who is the exact likeness of God.
⁵ You see, we don't go around preaching about ourselves. We preach that Jesus Christ is Lord, and we ourselves are your servants for Jesus' sake.
⁶ For God, who said, "Let there be light in the darkness," has made this light shine in our hearts so we could know the glory of God that is seen in the face of Jesus Christ.
⁷ We now have this light shining in our hearts, but we ourselves are like fragile clay jars containing this great treasure. This makes it clear that our great power is from God, not from ourselves.
⁸ We are pressed on every side by troubles, but we are not crushed. We are perplexed, but not driven to despair.
⁹ We are hunted down, but never abandoned by God. We get knocked down, but we are not destroyed.

[10] Through suffering, our bodies continue to share in the death of Jesus so that the life of Jesus may also be seen in our bodies.

Psalm 146:8 NLT: The Lord opens the eyes of the blind. The Lord lifts up those who are weighed down. The Lord loves the godly.

Jesus is the anchor of our soul who secures our soul just like he secures a ship. Jesus will not let believers be swept away by the strong powerful waves. Hebrews 6:19, CSB tell us:
[19] We have this hope as an anchor for the soul, firm and secure. It enters the inner sanctuary behind the curtain. 1 Peter 2:25 in the NLT says: Once you were like sheep who wandered away. But now you have turned to your Shepherd the Guardian of your souls.

I pray you apply some helpful tips, not to overload or over-stimulate your mind. Our brain requires rest and needs a mental break. Psalm 23:1-3 reads in the ESV:

1 The Lord is my shepherd, I lack nothing.

2   He makes me lie down in green pastures,

he leads me beside quiet waters,

3   he refreshes my soul.

He guides me along the right paths

for his name's sake.

Here are the tips I personally use myself to keep my peace of mind:

• Address your problem.

• Write down the solution.

• Come up with a plan.

- Take action.

- Stop making a mountain out of a molehill.

- Put things into a spiritual perspective.

- Ask yourself, what does the Bible say about my situation?

- Visualize all the things that are part of the solution.

- Turn off alerts and notifications on your phone.

- Set a time limit on problem solving.

- Try not to overstimulate your mind before bedtime.

- Stop multitasking, which overloads the brain.

- Write down a to-do-list and prioritize them into three different lists, first – urgent, second – very important, and third – important.

- Decide not to worry and overthink too much.

- Leave out "What if" thoughts, knowing our Heavenly Father fights for us. There is no need to have troubling, crippling, defeating thoughts.

Our soul becomes calmer and sharper when we pray like Jesus. We all need silence and solitude to keep our serenity. Mark 1:35-39, NIV explains:

> [35] Very early in the morning, while it was still dark, Jesus got up, left the house and went off to a solitary place, where he prayed.
> [36] Simon and his companions went to look for him,
> [37] and when they found him, they exclaimed: "Everyone is looking for you!"
> [38] Jesus replied, "Let us go somewhere else—to the nearby villages—so I can preach there also. That is why I have come."
> [39] So he traveled throughout Galilee, preaching in their synagogues and driving out demons.

Jesus knew He had to be alone with God, and it is the same for all believers. In Ephesians 6:18, NIV it says:

¹⁸ And pray in the Spirit on all occasions with all kinds of prayers and requests. With this in mind, be alert and always keep on praying for all the Lord's people.

A day without prayer is a day without power. ASAP stands for As Soon As Possible, but also stands for **A**lways **S**ay **A** **P**rayer.

The Holy Spirit does not want anyone's mind to be in the dark or have a depraved mindset. A depraved mind will never experience peace of mind or emotional freedom if the person does not have the attitude of Jesus. Ephesians 4:17-24, NIV says:

¹⁷ So I tell you this, and insist on it in the Lord, that you must no longer live as the Gentiles do, in the futility of their thinking.

¹⁸ They are darkened in their understanding and separated from the life of God because of the ignorance that is in them due to the hardening of their hearts.

¹⁹ Having lost all sensitivity, they have given themselves over to sensuality so as to indulge in every kind of impurity, and they are full of greed.

²⁰ That, however, is not the way of life you learned

²¹ when you heard about Christ and were taught in him in accordance with the truth that is in Jesus.

²² You were taught, with regard to your former way of life, to put off your old self, which is being corrupted by its deceitful desires;

²³ to be made new in the attitude of your minds;

²⁴ and to put on the new self, created to be like God in true righteousness and holiness.

Life not lived God's way is futile: The meaning of futility is pointlessness or uselessness. 2 Timothy 3:1-9, NIV reads:

¹But mark this: There will be terrible times in the last days.

² People will be lovers of themselves, lovers of money, boastful, proud, abusive, disobedient to their parents, ungrateful, unholy,

³ without love, unforgiving, slanderous, without self-control, brutal, not lovers of the good,

⁴ treacherous, rash, conceited, lovers of pleasure rather than lovers of God—

⁵ having a form of godliness but denying its power. Have nothing to do with such people.

⁶ They are the kind who worm their way into homes and gain control over gullible women, who are loaded down with sins and are swayed by all kinds of evil desires,

⁷ always learning but never able to come to a knowledge of the truth.

⁸ Just as Jannes and Jambres opposed Moses, so also these teachers oppose the truth. They are men of depraved minds, who, as far as the faith is concerned, are rejected.

⁹ But they will not get very far because, as in the case of those men, their folly will be clear to everyone.

Without the Lord mankind is depraved. Depraved means morally corrupt or wicked.

The Holy Spirit can give all believers a crystal clean mindset. 1 Peter 4:7, NIV:

⁷ The end of all things is near. Therefore be alert and of sober mind so that you may pray.

Let God free your soul and make you whole. God gives us hope to cope successfully. May you never lose your peace of mind. Always give God some time in prayer. Your mind is like a beautiful garden with bright colors. God wants all believers to keep a lovely, gorgeous garden free from weeds taking over. The weeds stand for negative thoughts, toxic thoughts, defeating thoughts, discouraging thoughts, or carnal thoughts. The meaning of carnal is relating to the appetites, passions of the body, and sensuality.

Our thoughts impact our life for victory or defeat. The Holy Spirit will give you bright ideas, creative ideas, fresh ideas, and positive ideas. You can live out your DVD, which stands for

Dreams

Visions

Desires.

I Hope you put on the attitude of Jesus every day.

CHAPTER 3 EMOTIONAL FREEDOM

It is very unhealthy to bear thoughts that cause unbearable emotional, hurtful, or painful feelings. God wants all believers to guard their heart. Proverbs 4:20-27, NLT explains,

[20] My child, pay attention to what I say. Listen carefully to my words.

[21] Don't lose sight of them. Let them penetrate deep into your heart,

[22] for they bring life to those who find them, and healing to their whole body.

[23] Guard your heart above all else, for it determines the course of your life.

[24] Avoid all perverse talk; stay away from corrupt speech.

[25] Look straight ahead, and fix your eyes on what lies before you.

[26] Mark out a straight path for your feet; stay on the safe path.

[27] Don't get sidetracked; keep your feet from following evil.

So, how does a believer guard their heart? The answer is simple. Do not let the devil enter the gates such as the eyes, ears, mind, heart, or sex outside of marriage.

Chapter Two explains the mindsets to guard your heart in further detail.

Our spiritual heart is dependent on a mental filter that takes every thought and aligns it up with the Word of God. In 2 Corinthians 10:5, NIV tells us to take captive every thought to make it obedient to Christ.

We demolish arguments and every pretension that sets itself up against the knowledge of God, and we take captive every thought to make it obedient to Christ.

Believers can trust God to guard their hearts and minds. The power of prayer keeps a believer's soul at peace. God instructs us how to think. The scriptures in Philippians 4:6-9, NLT, explain,

> [6] Don't worry about anything; instead, pray about everything. Tell God what you need, and thank him for all he has done. [7] Then you will experience God's peace, which exceeds anything we can understand. His peace will guard your hearts and minds as you live in Christ Jesus.
>
> [8] And now, dear brothers and sisters, one final thing. Fix your thoughts on what is true, and honorable, and right, and pure, and lovely, and admirable. Think about things that are excellent and worthy of praise. [9] Keep putting into practice all you learned and received from me—everything you heard from me and saw me doing. Then the God of peace will be with you.

The physical enemy in a war aims for the heart which is a vital organ to strike in order to kill people. Our spiritual enemy satan aims for the soul, which is the mind, and emotions. The helmet of salvation protects our mind so strongholds do not develop. This is for our spiritual protection. A stronghold is a way of thinking that develops within your soul to discourage you, disappoint you, keep you depressed, discontented, devastated, and in despair. Believers will not be destroyed when they think like the Bible tells them.

The Bible reveals this in 2 Corinthians 4:4-9, NIV:

> [4] Satan, who is the god of this world, has blinded the minds

of those who don't believe. They are unable to see the glorious light of the Good News. They don't understand this message about the glory of Christ, who is the exact likeness of God.

⁵ You see, we don't go around preaching about ourselves. We preach that Jesus Christ is Lord, and we ourselves are your servants for Jesus' sake. ⁶ For God, who said, "Let there be light in the darkness," has made this light shine in our hearts so we could know the glory of God that is seen in the face of Jesus Christ.

⁷ We now have this light shining in our hearts, but we ourselves are like fragile clay jars containing this great treasure.[a] This makes it clear that our great power is from God, not from ourselves.

⁸ We are pressed on every side by troubles, but we are not crushed. We are perplexed, but not driven to despair. ⁹ We are hunted down, but never abandoned by God. We get knocked down, but we are not destroyed.

Psalm 146:8, NLT reads:

⁸The Lord opens the eyes of the blind. The Lord lifts up those who are weighed down. The Lord loves the godly.

The devil loves to destroy and devour. Scripture says in John 10:10, NKJV, and 1 Peter 5:6-9, NKJV

¹⁰ The thief does not come except to steal, and to kill, and to destroy. I have come that they may have life, and that they may have *it* more abundantly.

⁶ Therefore humble yourselves under the mighty hand of God, that He may exalt you in due time, ⁷ casting all your care upon Him, for He cares for you.

⁸ Be sober, be vigilant; because your adversary the devil walks about like a roaring lion, seeking whom he may devour. ⁹ Resist him, steadfast in the faith, knowing that the same sufferings are experienced by your brotherhood in the world.

The devil wants to weaken your faith by you not guarding your mind. Let me give you some meaning of some words in these scriptures.

Sober implies mentally alert and self-controlled.

Vigilant means watchful, awake, and alert.

Resist means to stand up to him and be firm.

Steadfast means standing firm without moving even under an attack from the enemy.

Studies have proven to never turn your back on a charging lion and run, because standing firm and facing them confuses them. Most of the time the lion will turn another way.

Believers' greatest defense is to be humble and live in a right relationship with God. James 4:7 NLT tells us:

> ⁷ So humble yourselves before God. Resist the devil, and he will flee from you.

Now let's see James 4:7 in the NIV, which reads

> ⁷ Submit yourselves, then, to God. Resist the devil, and he will flee from you.

To submit means to put ourself under God's authority. The scripture in Luke 10:19, NIV tells us nothing will harm us.

> ¹⁹ I have given you authority to trample on snakes and scorpions and to overcome all the power of the enemy; nothing will harm you.

Believers must believe God will fight for them and the battle belongs to the Lord. No matter what you are going through, God's battle plan looks nothing like man's. God's ways are higher to manage stress in life. He gives believer's victory. He gave the Israelites victory and got all of them through the Red Sea, and all the Egyptians drowned.

Guarding our hearts is easy when we put on the attitude of Jesus and think like Jesus, as I mentioned in Chapter Two.

Scriptures tell us in Proverbs 4:20-27, NLT:

²⁰My child, pay attention to what I say. Listen carefully to my words.

²¹ Don't lose sight of them. Let them penetrate deep into your heart,

²² for they bring life to those who find them, and healing to their whole body.

²³ Guard your heart above all else, for it determines the course of your life.

²⁴ Avoid all perverse talk; stay away from corrupt speech.

²⁵ Look straight ahead, and fix your eyes on what lies before you.

²⁶ Mark out a straight path for your feet; stay on the safe path.

²⁷ Don't get sidetracked; keep your feet from following evil.

Remember the five gates the devil tries to enter in to destroy our soul and body. Those five gates are, our mind, emotions, eyes, ears, and sex outside of marriage.

The devil cannot destroy our soul when we have the helmet of salvation on because it protects our mind. The devil cannot destroy our hearts when we have the breastplate of righteousness because it protects our heart.

God's Supernatural Power protects our soul. In Ephesians 6:10-18, NLT, it reads,

¹⁰ A final word: Be strong in the Lord and in his mighty power.
¹¹ Put on all of God's armor so that you will be able to stand firm against all strategies of the devil.
¹² For we are not fighting against flesh-and-blood enemies, but against evil rulers and authorities of the unseen world, against mighty powers in this dark world, and against evil spirits in the heavenly places.
¹³ Therefore, put on every piece of God's armor so you will be able to resist the enemy in the time of evil. Then after the

battle you will still be standing firm.

¹⁴ Stand your ground, putting on the belt of truth and the body armor of God's righteousness.

¹⁵ For shoes, put on the peace that comes from the Good News so that you will be fully prepared.

¹⁶ In addition to all of these, hold up the shield of faith to stop the fiery arrows of the devil

¹⁷ Put on salvation as your helmet, and take the sword of the Spirit, which is the word of God.

¹⁸ Pray in the Spirit at all times and on every occasion. Stay alert and be persistent in your prayers for all believers everywhere

Paul was in prison in Rome when he wrote this letter. Paul got a spiritual message on the breastplate of righteousness as he studied the Roman soldiers. The breastplate of righteousness protected the soldiers' heart from physical injury, but also protects our tender heart.

The Holy Spirit protects our hearts from the attacks from the enemy. The breastplate of righteousness and the shield of faith protect our hearts, Matthew 5:6, ESV:

⁶ "Blessed are those who hunger and thirst for righteousness, for they shall be satisfied.

Believers can laugh at the fiery darts, knowing the darts cannot penetrate our hearts.

The fires of the explosive darts were quenched because the Roman soldiers soaked the leather shield in water. The Holy Spirit does not want believers to quench the Holy Spirit's fire when our hearts are troubled. The Spirit comes to us as a fire and gives us freedom in our soul. The Holy Spirit wants to inflame our hearts with His supernatural indwelling power.

In 1 Thessalonians 5:19, ESV, it tells us "Do not quench the Spirit."

The devil loves to keep toxic emotions deep within so it prevents you from giving God all of your heart. The devil loves when a person is filled with unpleasant toxic feelings such as anger, bitterness, fear, guilt, hate, or unforgiveness.

The first toxic emotion is **<u>Anger</u>**. The best scripture to start with can be found in Ephesians 4:26-27, NLT:

> 26 And "don't sin by letting anger control you."[a] Don't let the sun go down while you are still angry, 27 for anger gives a foothold to the devil.

Do you agree the sun goes down every evening? I hope you agreed so, in so many words we should never go to bed angry to give the devil a foothold. A foothold is a place where a person's foot can be lodged to support them securely. The longer a person lets anger linger, it develops a foothold deep within your heart. The enemy loves when anger burns within the heart.

God does not want your foot to slip, slide, or sink. Your foot is part of your body and God does not want you to fall. The Roman soldiers' footwear in the early first century put studs on the bottom of their sandals to prevent them from falling to get a better grip in battle to fight better.

In Matthew 7:24-27, ESV, it talks about a physical house being built, but also gives a spiritual message for the house the Holy Spirit lives in which is our body.

> 24 "Everyone then who hears these words of mine and does them will be like a wise man who built his house on the rock.

> 25 And the rain fell, and the floods came, and the winds blew and beat on that house, but it did not fall, because it had been founded on the rock.

> 26 And everyone who hears these words of mine and does not do them will be like a foolish man who built his house on the sand.

> 27 And the rain fell, and the floods came, and the winds blew and beat against that house, and it fell, and great was the fall of it."

1 John 4:4, in the NKJV, says "You are of God, little children, and have overcome them, because He who is in you is greater

than he who is in the world."

The devil gets joy and wants you to sink with anger in your heart over your situation. John 10:10, NKJV, tells us:

> ¹⁰ The thief does not come except to steal, and to kill, and to destroy. I have come that they may have life, and that they may have *it* more abundantly.

The Bible tells us people that have out-of-control anger are fools in Proverbs 29:11, NLT:

> ¹¹Fools vent their anger, but the wise quietly hold it back.

Scriptures give us wisdom to manage anger wisely. In Proverbs 15:1, ESV, it explains

> ¹A soft answer turns away wrath, but a harsh word stirs up anger.

I love Thomas Jefferson saying "When angry count to ten. If very angry count to one hundred." When the heat of anger arises within, just freeze until you cool down!

Guarding our heart is wise because toxic emotions destroy our soul and body. According to better health channel, unmanaged or unresolved anger causes high blood pressure, heart attack, stroke, headache, abdominal pain, depression, digestive problems, skin problems, insomnia, and increased anxiety.

God wants us to guard our hearts so stress hormones do not damage our body He wants our soul to prosper as we gain knowledge. Scripture tells us in 3 John 2, NKJV,

> ² Beloved, I pray that you may prosper in all things and be in health, just as your soul prospers.

God warned Cain about his anger. God knew Gain's anger was headed towards the danger zone. The Bible explains the story in Genesis 4:1-15, ESV:

> **4** Now Adam knew Eve his wife, and she conceived and bore Cain, saying, "I have gotten[a] a man with the help of the Lord."

² And again, she bore his brother Abel. Now Abel was a keeper of sheep, and Cain a worker of the ground.

³ In the course of time Cain brought to the Lord an offering of the fruit of the ground,

⁴ and Abel also brought of the firstborn of his flock and of their fat portions. And the Lord had regard for Abel and his offering,

⁵ but for Cain and his offering he had no regard. So Cain was very angry, and his face fell.

⁶ The Lord said to Cain, "Why are you angry, and why has your face fallen?

⁷ If you do well, will you not be accepted? And if you do not do well, sin is crouching at the door. Its desire is contrary to you, but you must rule over it."

⁸ Cain spoke to Abel his brother. And when they were in the field, Cain rose up against his brother Abel and killed him.

⁹ Then the Lord said to Cain, "Where is Abel your brother?" He said, "I do not know; am I my brother's keeper?"

¹⁰ And the Lord said, "What have you done? The voice of your brother's blood is crying to me from the ground.

¹¹ And now you are cursed from the ground, which has opened its mouth to receive your brother's blood from your hand.

¹² When you work the ground, it shall no longer yield to you its strength. You shall be a fugitive and a wanderer on the earth."

¹³ Cain said to the Lord, "My punishment is greater than I can bear.

¹⁴ Behold, you have driven me today away from the ground, and from your face I shall be hidden. I shall be a fugitive and a wanderer on the earth, and whoever finds me will kill me."

¹⁵ Then the Lord said to him, "Not so! If anyone kills Cain, vengeance shall be taken on him sevenfold." And the Lord put a mark on Cain, lest any who found him should at-

tack him.

God knew the heart of Cain, but Cain did not take godly advice. God was trying to get Cain to express his anger, but Cain had silent anger. Cain's jealous heart turned into bitterness which led him into having a hostile heart, and he killed an innocent family member. Cain's emotional reasoning overruled his rational thoughts.

The Word of God says in Jeremiah 17:9-10, ESV,

> [9]The heart is deceitful above all things, and desperately sick; who can understand it?
>
> [10] "I the Lord search the heart and test the mind, to give every man according to his ways, according to the fruit of his deeds."

God had mercy for Cain. He protected a sinner. God is so gracious and shows divine grace with His unconditional love.

By renewing our mind with the Word of God, our heart is purged of evil and is filled with God's truth. Purged means to have a pure, clean, holy and righteous heart and mindset. Luke 6:45 ESV,

> [45] The good person out of the good treasure of his heart produces good, and the evil person out of his evil treasure produces evil, for out of the abundance of the heart his mouth speaks.

The mind speaks from the heart. The Bible tells us to put on the attitude of Jesus so our heart does not deceive us. In Proverbs 23:7, in The Bible in Basic English, reads, "For as the thoughts of his heart are, so is he: Take food and drink, he says to you; but his heart is not with you."

Just because you're eating at the expense of others does not mean everyone has their heart for your best interest on a:

• Relationship decision
• Business decision
• Investment decision
• Political decision

- Retirement decision
- Moving decision
- Job decision
- Family decision
- Church decision
- Wedding decision
- College decision

Psalm 1, 1-2, NIV, reads:

> [1] Blessed is the one who does not walk in step with the wicked or stand in the way that sinners take or sit in the company of mockers,
>
> [2] but whose delight is in the law of the Lord, and who meditates on his law day and night.

God had Cain's best interest in His heart for Cain, but Cain's anger dominated him to make the wrong decision.

The Bible explains about getting rid of anger in Ephesians 4:31-32, NIV:

> [31] Get rid of all bitterness, rage and anger, brawling and slander, along with every form of malice.
>
> [32] Be kind and compassionate to one another, forgiving each other, just as in Christ God forgave you.

Malice means the intention or desire to do evil. **Right anger** is justified anger and is always disciplined and controlled to correct a situation in the most peaceful way.

John 2:13-16, NIV, is a great illustration – it speaks on Jesus overturning tables.

> [13] When it was almost time for the Jewish Passover, Jesus went up to Jerusalem.
>
> [14] In the temple courts he found people selling cattle, sheep and doves, and others sitting at tables exchanging money.
>
> [15] So he made a whip out of cords, and drove all from the temple courts, both sheep and cattle; he scattered the coins of the money changers and overturned their tables.

16 To those who sold doves he said, "Get these out of here! Stop turning my Father's house into a market!"

Wrong anger is unjustified anger. It will not forget; it lingers to fester in a person's soul like deadly poison. This anger seeks to destroy and seeks revenge.

Another person in the Bible with deep anger was King Saul.

First Samuel 18:1-12, NLT, tells us about King Saul's anger turned into deep jealousy over David.

> **1** After David had finished talking with Saul, he met Jonathan, the king's son. There was an immediate bond between them, for Jonathan loved David.
> **2** From that day on Saul kept David with him and wouldn't let him return home.
> **3** And Jonathan made a solemn pact with David, because he loved him as he loved himself.
> **4** Jonathan sealed the pact by taking off his robe and giving it to David, together with his tunic, sword, bow, and belt.
> **5** Whatever Saul asked David to do, David did it successfully. So Saul made him a commander over the men of war, an appointment that was welcomed by the people and Saul's officers alike.
> **6** When the victorious Israelite army was returning home after David had killed the Philistine, women from all the towns of Israel came out to meet King Saul. They sang and danced for joy with tambourines and cymbals.
> **7** This was their song: "Saul has killed his thousands, and David his ten thousands!"
> **8** This made Saul very angry. "What's this?" he said. "They credit David with ten thousands and me with only thousands. Next they'll be making him their king!"
> **9** So from that time on Saul kept a jealous eye on David.
> **10** The very next day a tormenting spirit from God overwhelmed Saul, and he began to rave in his house like a madman. David was playing the harp, as he did each day. But

Saul had a spear in his hand,

[11] and he suddenly hurled it at David, intending to pin him to the wall. But David escaped him twice.

[12] Saul was then afraid of David, for the Lord was with David and had turned away from Saul.

King Saul tried to kill David at least 12 times. David highly respected King Saul and spared Saul's life two times. See, David had a conscience of right and wrong. He had the right spiritual thoughts. David was a man after God's own heart. First Samuel 24:1-21, NLT:

[1] After Saul returned from fighting the Philistines, he was told that David had gone into the wilderness of En-gedi.

[2] So Saul chose 3,000 elite troops from all Israel and went to search for David and his men near the rocks of the wild goats.

[3] At the place where the road passes some sheepfolds, Saul went into a cave to relieve himself. But as it happened, David and his men were hiding farther back in that very cave!

[4] "Now's your opportunity!" David's men whispered to him. "Today the Lord is telling you, 'I will certainly put your enemy into your power, to do with as you wish.'" So David crept forward and cut off a piece of the hem of Saul's robe.

[5] But then David's conscience began bothering him because he had cut Saul's robe.

[6] He said to his men, "The Lord forbid that I should do this to my lord the king. I shouldn't attack the Lord's anointed one, for the Lord himself has chosen him."

[7] So David restrained his men and did not let them kill Saul. After Saul had left the cave and gone on his way,

[8] David came out and shouted after him, "My lord the king!" And when Saul looked around, David bowed low before him.

[9] Then he shouted to Saul, "Why do you listen to the people who say I am trying to harm you?

10 This very day you can see with your own eyes it isn't true. For the Lord placed you at my mercy back there in the cave. Some of my men told me to kill you, but I spared you. For I said, 'I will never harm the king—he is the Lord's anointed one.'

11 Look, my father, at what I have in my hand. It is a piece of the hem of your robe! I cut it off, but I didn't kill you. This proves that I am not trying to harm you and that I have not sinned against you, even though you have been hunting for me to kill me.

12 "May the Lord judge between us. Perhaps the Lord will punish you for what you are trying to do to me, but I will never harm you.

13 As that old proverb says, 'From evil people come evil deeds.' So you can be sure I will never harm you.

14 Who is the king of Israel trying to catch anyway? Should he spend his time chasing one who is as worthless as a dead dog or a single flea?

15 May the Lord therefore judge which of us is right and punish the guilty one. He is my advocate, and he will rescue me from your power!"

16 When David had finished speaking, Saul called back, "Is that really you, my son David?" Then he began to cry.

17 And he said to David, "You are a better man than I am, for you have repaid me good for evil.

18 Yes, you have been amazingly kind to me today, for when the Lord put me in a place where you could have killed me, you didn't do it.

19 Who else would let his enemy get away when he had him in his power? May the Lord reward you well for the kindness you have shown me today.

20 And now I realize that you are surely going to be king, and that the kingdom of Israel will flourish under your rule.

21 Now swear to me by the Lord that when that happens you will not kill my family and destroy my line of descendants!"

David had mercy on King Saul and God had mercy on Cain.

The difference between Cain and David was, Cain had silent anger but David knew how to express his anger. David expressed himself and wrote Psalm 142 NLT in prayer when King Saul was out to kill him. Remember in 1 Samuel 24:3, Saul and David hid in the same cave. This is what David says in Psalm 142, NLT,

[1]I cry out to the Lord; I plead for the Lord's mercy.

[2] I pour out my complaints before him and tell him all my troubles.

[3] When I am overwhelmed, you alone know the way I should turn. Wherever I go,
   my enemies have set traps for me.

[4] I look for someone to come and help me, but no one gives me a passing thought!
No one will help me; no one cares a bit what happens to me.

[5] Then I pray to you, O Lord. I say, "You are my place of refuge. You are all I really want in life.

[6] Hear my cry, for I am very low. Rescue me from my persecutors, for they are too strong for me.

[7] Bring me out of prison so I can thank you. The godly will crowd around me, for you are good to me."

The Bible gives us wisdom to manage anger successfully. It tells us in James 1:19-20, NLT:

> [19] Understand this, my dear brothers and sisters: You must all be quick to listen, slow to speak, and slow to get angry. [20] Human anger[a] does not produce the righteousness[b] God desires.

I have quoted this verse a few times but it bears repeating. A major part of walking in freedom is self control over what you speak.

To be quick to listen means to receive the Word that saves your soul, which requires concentration.

Slow to speak means do not blurt out while another person is speaking.

Slow to become angry means do not react against God's Word of righteousness.

God wants to give you emotional freedom from toxic feelings. James 1:25, NLT, reads:

> [25] But if you look carefully into the perfect law that sets you free, and if you do what it says and don't forget what you heard, then God will bless you for doing it.

Remember the six top toxic emotions are anger, bitterness, fear, guilt, hate, and unforgiveness.

God gives all believers emotional freedom not to be distracted by the worldly affairs here on earth.

So to be slow to anger one must not lash out harsh words which only leads to guilt, shame, and regrets.

The Bible tells us many times that our Heavenly Father and Jesus were slow to anger in Psalm 103:8-14, NLT:

> [8] The Lord is compassionate and merciful, slow to get angry and filled with unfailing love.

⁹ He will not constantly accuse us, nor remain angry forever.

¹⁰ He does not punish us for all our sins; he does not deal harshly with us, as we deserve.

¹¹ For his unfailing love toward those who fear him is as great as the height of the heavens above the earth.

¹² He has removed our sins as far from us as the east is from the west.

¹³ The Lord is like a father to his children, tender and compassionate to those who fear him.

¹⁴ For he knows how weak we are; he remembers we are only dust.

Jesus did not have a sinful nature like ours. The Holy Spirit's redeeming power can transform us from human nature to divine nature to manage unpleasant toxic feelings.

2 Peter 1:3-9, NLT, explains it very simply:

³ By his divine power, God has given us everything we need for living a godly life. We have received all of this by coming to know him, the one who called us to himself by means of his marvelous glory and excellence.

⁴ And because of his glory and excellence, he has given us great and precious promises. These are the promises that enable you to share his divine nature and escape the world's corruption caused by human desires.

⁵ In view of all this, make every effort to respond to God's promises. Supplement your faith with a generous provision of moral excellence, and moral excellence with knowledge,

⁶ and knowledge with self-control, and self-control with patient endurance, and patient endurance with godliness,

⁷ and godliness with brotherly affection, and brotherly affection with love for everyone.

⁸ The more you grow like this, the more productive and useful you will be in your knowledge of our Lord Jesus Christ.

⁹ But those who fail to develop in this way are shortsighted

or blind, forgetting that they have been cleansed from their old sins.

There are two ways some people manage anger, which are anger <u>avoiders</u> and anger <u>exploders</u>.

<u>Anger avoiders</u> try to keep the peace at all cost and suppress his or her anger. Some avoiders are afraid of how others are going to respond or are scared of losing control themselves.

<u>Anger exploders</u> express anger too freely; they are like a volcano most of the time ready to erupt. This can cause hurt and harm to others.

The Bible tells us about outbursts of anger in Galatians 5:19-26, NLT:

> [19] When you follow the desires of your sinful nature, the results are very clear: sexual immorality, impurity, lustful pleasures,
>
> [20] idolatry, sorcery, hostility, quarreling, jealousy, outbursts of anger, selfish ambition, dissension, division,
>
> [21] envy, drunkenness, wild parties, and other sins like these. Let me tell you again, as I have before, that anyone living that sort of life will not inherit the Kingdom of God.
>
> [22] But the Holy Spirit produces this kind of fruit in our lives: love, joy, peace, patience, kindness, goodness, faithfulness,
>
> [23] gentleness, and self-control. There is no law against these things!
>
> [24] Those who belong to Christ Jesus have nailed the passions and desires of their sinful nature to his cross and crucified them there.
>
> [25] Since we are living by the Spirit, let us follow the Spirit's leading in every part of our lives.
>
> [26] Let us not become conceited, or provoke one another, or be jealous of one another.

Remember Cain was angry and jealous over his brother and killed him.

King Saul was angry and jealous over David's success and

tried to kill him over 12 times.

Jesus was a pro managing anger when he was hung on the cross and paid the penalty for our sins. We can tell by some words he used. Luke 23:34, ESV:

[34] And Jesus said, "Father, forgive them, for they know not what they do." And they cast lots to divide his garments.

Jesus forgave instantly.

John 19:30, ESV

[30] When Jesus had received the sour wine, he said, "It is finished," and he bowed his head and gave up his spirit.

This scripture means triumph. Jesus was victorious doing our Heavenly Father's will.
Jesus had a divine nature and always responded in the Spirit.

As believers we need to be wise with our words when solving conflict. It is wise to use "I am angry" statements instead of "you make me angry."

Stay away from fighting words such as "you always," "you never." Use calmer words such as "seldom" or "sometimes," to quench the fire of anger.

Proverbs 15:1,4 reads:

[1]A gentle answer deflects anger, but harsh words make tempers flare.

[4]Gentle words are a tree of life; a deceitful tongue crushes the spirit.

and Proverbs 29:11, NLT, which reads:

[11]Fools vent their anger, but the wise quietly hold it back.

Here are some phrases to say under your breath as you are listening to words from the evil one that try to make you angry.
· Help me Lord
· Calm Down
· Peace Be Still

Let me share one last story about hotheaded Peter in Luke 22:47-51, NLT:

47 But even as Jesus said this, a crowd approached, led by Judas, one of the twelve disciples. Judas walked over to Jesus to greet him with a kiss.

48 But Jesus said, "Judas, would you betray the Son of Man with a kiss?"

49 When the other disciples saw what was about to happen, they exclaimed, "Lord, should we fight? We brought the swords!"

50 And one of them struck at the high priest's slave, slashing off his right ear.

51 But Jesus said, "No more of this." And he touched the man's ear and healed him.

In John 18:10, NLT, the same story is told which gives the name Peter.

10 Then Simon Peter drew a sword and slashed off the right ear of Malchus, the high priest's slave.

Managing anger will prevent a lot of heartaches, and regrets.

Some people get an emotional rush when they are out of control to gain control of a person or others.

The Bible tells us in Proverbs 22:24, in the Message Bible, "Don't hang out with angry people; don't keep company with hotheads."

The main scripture on anger is found in Ephesians 4:26-27, NLT says:

26 And "don't sin by letting anger control you."[a] Don't let the sun go down while you are still angry,

27 for anger gives a foothold to the devil.

The root causes of some anger include hurt, pain, rejection, and humiliation.

Jesus experienced all four but was not filled with rage dying on the cross.

As believers with the Holy Spirit's help we can choose the following steps to manage anger successfully.

• Respond like Jesus with Holy anger.
• Do not personalize the other person's unkind, crude words.
• Tell the other person in private, I did not appreciate you putting me down or criticizing me.
• Leave quickly if anger is rising up within your heart. Say "we can discuss this later, I am not ready to talk right now."
• Do not retaliate. God says "Vengeance is mine."

Some people who humiliate others are carnal minded to make themselves feel powerful. They do not have the attitude of Jesus I mentioned in Chapter Two.

Some people have unresolved anger and overreact on minor issues. This I call misplaced anger, taking out on innocent people.

Believers are alive in Christ and our Soulish being does not dominate or control us when we became Born Again.

Ephesians 2:1-10, NLT, explains it very well, which says,

[1]Once you were dead because of your disobedience and your many sins.

[2] You used to live in sin, just like the rest of the world, obeying the devil—the commander of the powers in the unseen world. He is the spirit at work in the hearts of those who refuse to obey God.

[3] All of us used to live that way, following the passionate desires and inclinations of our sinful nature. By our very nature we were subject to God's anger, just like everyone else.

[4] But God is so rich in mercy, and he loved us so much,

[5] that even though we were dead because of our sins, he gave us life when he raised Christ from the dead. (It is only by God's grace that you have been saved!)

[6] For he raised us from the dead along with Christ and seated us with him in the heavenly realms because we are

united with Christ Jesus.

⁷ So God can point to us in all future ages as examples of the incredible wealth of his grace and kindness toward us, as shown in all he has done for us who are united with Christ Jesus.

⁸ God saved you by his grace when you believed. And you can't take credit for this; it is a gift from God.

⁹ Salvation is not a reward for the good things we have done, so none of us can boast about it.

¹⁰ For we are God's masterpiece. He has created us anew in Christ Jesus, so we can do the good things he planned for us long ago.

As followers of Jesus we have His divine new nature that unbelievers do not understand unless we share the salvation message. The Bible tells us about this new nature in Colossians 3:1-10, NLT, and 2 Corinthians 5:17-21, says:

¹Since you have been raised to new life with Christ, set your sights on the realities of heaven, where Christ sits in the place of honor at God's right hand.

² Think about the things of heaven, not the things of earth.

³ For you died to this life, and your real life is hidden with Christ in God.

⁴ And when Christ, who is your life, is revealed to the whole world, you will share in all his glory.

⁵ So put to death the sinful, earthly things lurking within you. Have nothing to do with sexual immorality, impurity, lust, and evil desires. Don't be greedy, for a greedy person is an idolater, worshiping the things of this world.

⁶ Because of these sins, the anger of God is coming.

⁷ You used to do these things when your life was still part of this world.

⁸ But now is the time to get rid of anger, rage, malicious be-havior, slander, and dirty language.

⁹ Don't lie to each other, for you have stripped off your old sinful nature and all its wicked deeds.

¹⁰ Put on your new nature, and be renewed as you learn to

know your Creator and become like him.

17 This means that anyone who belongs to Christ has become a new person. The old life is gone; a new life has begun!
18 And all of this is a gift from God, who brought us back to himself through Christ. And God has given us this task of reconciling people to him.
19 For God was in Christ, reconciling the world to himself, no longer counting people's sins against them. And he gave us this wonderful message of reconciliation.
20 So we are Christ's ambassadors; God is making his appeal through us. We speak for Christ when we plead, "Come back to God!"
21 For God made Christ, who never sinned, to be the offering for our sin,[a] so that we could be made right with God through Christ.

Paul wrote in 2 Corinthians 6:1-2, not to reject the salvation

1 As God's partners, we beg you not to accept this marvelous gift of God's kindness and then ignore it.
2 For God says, "At just the right time, I heard you. On the day of salvation, I helped you."

Indeed, the "right time" is now. Today is the day of salvation.

Salvation is deliverance from sin and its consequences which include death and separation from God.

Are you ready to give your life to our true Savior of the World? If so, say this simple prayer.
Heavenly Father, I know I am a sinner in need of a true Savior. I ask you to forgive me of my sins. I believe you died for my sins and rose from the dead. I ask you, Lord, to come into my heart and I want to trust and follow you as my Lord and Savior.

Angels are rejoicing right now over one sinner who repents. Welcome into the family of God.

Our sinful nature can never be successful managing toxic feelings unless we depend on God's divine nature, which is the Supreme Being.

Our Lord and Savior is slow to anger and is a righteous, honest, respectful judge. In Numbers 14:18, NLT, it tells us:

> [18] 'The Lord is slow to anger and filled with unfailing love, forgiving every kind of sin and rebellion. But he does not excuse the guilty. He lays the sins of the parents upon their children; the entire family is affected—even children in the third and fourth generations.'

God was angry at the mistreatment of others and the Israelites worshipping the golden calf. Both stories are found in Exodus 22:22-24, NLT, and Exodus 32:7-10, NLT.

> [22] "You must not exploit a widow or an orphan.
>
> [23] If you exploit them in any way and they cry out to me, then I will certainly hear their cry.
>
> [24] My anger will blaze against you, and I will kill you with the sword. Then your wives will be widows and your children fatherless.

Exodus 32:7-10 in the NLT says:

> [7] The Lord told Moses, "Quick! Go down the mountain! Your people whom you brought from the land of Egypt have corrupted themselves.
> [8] How quickly they have turned away from the way I commanded them to live! They have melted down gold and made a calf, and they have bowed down and sacrificed to it. They are saying, 'These are your gods, O Israel, who brought you out of the land of Egypt.'"
> [9] Then the Lord said, "I have seen how stubborn and rebellious these people are.
> [10] Now leave me alone so my fierce anger can blaze against them, and I will destroy them. Then I will make you, Moses, into a great nation."

One question, how would you write out your anger message by starting your writing with "I am angry because…"

In Romans 12:16-21, NLT, helps all believers to conserve their energy to not let anger control them.

16 Live in harmony with each other. Don't be too proud to enjoy the company of ordinary people. And don't think you know it all!

17 Never pay back evil with more evil. Do things in such a way that everyone can see you are honorable. 18 Do all that you can to live in peace with everyone.

19 Dear friends, never take revenge. Leave that to the righteous anger of God. For the Scriptures say, "I will take revenge; I will pay them back," says the Lord.

20 Instead, "If your enemies are hungry, feed them. If they are thirsty, give them something to drink. in doing this, you will heap burning coals of shame on their heads."

21 Don't let evil conquer you, but conquer evil by doing good.

The second toxic emotion that harms the soul and body is **Bitterness.** Bitterness does not have to take root in your heart if you deal with your hurt and anger God's way.
In Hebrews 12:11-15, ESV:

11 For the moment all discipline seems painful rather than pleasant, but later it yields the peaceful fruit of righteousness to those who have been trained by it.

12 Therefore lift your drooping hands and strengthen your weak knees,

13 and make straight paths for your feet, so that what is lame may not be put out of joint but rather be healed.

14 Strive for peace with everyone, and for the holiness without which no one will see the Lord.

15 See to it that no one fails to obtain the grace of God; that

no "root of bitterness" springs up and causes trouble, and by it many become defiled;

Defile means to corrupt or pollute, to make unclean or impure.

Anger that turns into bitterness is very destructive, that can destroy relationships in families, friends, and affect your health. Emotional pain that is not expressed poisons the soul. All believers have a choice to get better and not bitter.

Listen to Naomi's story in the Bible, whose name means pleasant but Naomi became bitter after losing her husband and two sons.

In the days when the judges ruled in Israel, a severe famine came upon the land. So a man from Bethlehem in Judah left his home and went to live in the country of Moab, taking his wife and two sons with him.

To sum up chapter 1 in Ruth, Naomi's husband died during their stay in Moab. Naomi's both sons died ten years later. Naomi decided to go back to her home town because she heard Judah was giving out good crops. Naomi encouraged both of her daughters-in-law to go back to their parent's home.

Ruth 1:13, part b-22, NLT,

my daughters! Things are far more bitter for me than for you, because the Lord himself has raised his fist against me."
14 And again they wept together, and Orpah kissed her mother-in-law good-bye. But Ruth clung tightly to Naomi.
15 "Look," Naomi said to her, "your sister-in-law has gone back to her people and to her gods. You should do the same."
16 But Ruth replied, "Don't ask me to leave you and turn back. Wherever you go, I will go; wherever you live, I will live. Your people will be my people, and your God will be my God.

^{17} Wherever you die, I will die, and there I will be buried. May the Lord punish me severely if I allow anything but death to separate us!"

^{18} When Naomi saw that Ruth was determined to go with her, she said nothing more.

^{19} So the two of them continued on their journey. When they came to Bethlehem, the entire town was excited by their arrival. "Is it really Naomi?" the women asked.

^{20} "Don't call me Naomi," she responded. "Instead, call me Mara, for the Almighty has made life very bitter for me.

^{21} I went away full, but the Lord has brought me home empty. Why call me Naomi when the Lord has caused me to suffer[b] and the Almighty has sent such tragedy upon me?"

^{22} So Naomi returned from Moab, accompanied by her daughter-in-law Ruth, the young Moabite woman. They arrived in Bethlehem in late spring, at the beginning of the barley harvest.

Naomi blamed God two times for her bitter attitude. She thought God was against her. In Ruth 1:13 in the ESV reads, "... No my daughters, for it is exceedingly bitter to me for your sake that the hand of the Lord has gone out against me." It is always wise to have a pray party instead of a pity party. God is not against anyone who lost someone they deeply loved. Our earthly bodies will not last forever but they will when we get our heavenly bodies.

The Bible speaks about our earthly bodies in 2 Corinthians 5:1-10, NLT:

^{1}For we know that when this earthly tent we live in is taken down (that is, when we die and leave this earthly body), we will have a house in heaven, an eternal body made for us by God himself and not by human hands.

^{2} We grow weary in our present bodies, and we long to put on our heavenly bodies like new clothing.

^{3} For we will put on heavenly bodies; we will not be spirits without bodies.[a]

^{4} While we live in these earthly bodies, we groan and sigh, but it's not that we want to die and get rid of these bodies that clothe us. Rather, we want to put on our new bodies so that these dying bodies will be swallowed up by life.

[5] God himself has prepared us for this, and as a guarantee he has given us his Holy Spirit.

[6] So we are always confident, even though we know that as long as we live in these bodies we are not at home with the Lord.

[7] For we live by believing and not by seeing.

[8] Yes, we are fully confident, and we would rather be away from these earthly bodies, for then we will be at home with the Lord.

[9] So whether we are here in this body or away from this body, our goal is to please him.

[10] For we must all stand before Christ to be judged. We will each receive whatever we deserve for the good or evil we have done in this earthly body.

Now let me read 2 Corinthians 4:16, NLT:

[16] That is why we never give up. Though our bodies are dying, our spirits are being renewed every day.

We will all leave this earth one day. Ruth seemed like she managed her emotional pain better than Naomi. Ruth was confident she would have favor on the field to provide food for Naomi and herself.

In Ruth 2:1-2, ESV says:

[1] Now Naomi had a relative of her husband's, a worthy man of the clan of Elimelech, whose name was Boaz.

[2] And Ruth the Moabite said to Naomi, "Let me go to the field and glean among the ears of grain after him in whose sight I shall find favor." And she said to her, "Go, my daughter."

Now, Boaz knew who Ruth was because his workers told him. She found favor, it explains in Ruth 2:8-16, ESV reads:

[8] Then Boaz said to Ruth, "Now, listen, my daughter, do not

go to glean in another field or leave this one, but keep close to my young women.

⁹ Let your eyes be on the field that they are reaping, and go after them. Have I not charged the young men not to touch you? And when you are thirsty, go to the vessels and drink what the young men have drawn."

¹⁰ Then she fell on her face, bowing to the ground, and said to him, "Why have I found favor in your eyes, that you should take notice of me, since I am a foreigner?"

¹¹ But Boaz answered her, "All that you have done for your mother-in-law since the death of your husband has been fully told to me, and how you left your father and mother and your native land and came to a people that you did not know before.

¹² The Lord repay you for what you have done, and a full reward be given you by the Lord, the God of Israel, under whose wings you have come to take refuge!"

¹³ Then she said, "I have found favor in your eyes, my lord, for you have comforted me and spoken kindly to your servant, though I am not one of your servants."

¹⁴ And at mealtime Boaz said to her, "Come here and eat some bread and dip your morsel in the wine." So she sat beside the reapers, and he passed to her roasted grain. And she ate until she was satisfied, and she had some left over.

¹⁵ When she rose to glean, Boaz instructed his young men, saying, "Let her glean even among the sheaves, and do not reproach her.

¹⁶ And also pull out some from the bundles for her and leave it for her to glean, and do not rebuke her."

Boaz blesses Ruth again it tells us in Ruth 3:16-17, ESV:

¹⁶ And when she came to her mother-in-law, she said, "How did you fare, my daughter?" Then she told her all that the man had done for her,

¹⁷ saying, "These six measures of barley he gave to me, for he said to me, 'You must not go back empty-handed to your

mother-in-law.'"

God is a man of His Promise. Philippians 4:19, ESV, reads:

> [19] And my God will supply every need of yours according to his riches in glory in Christ Jesus.

At the end of this story Naomi and Ruth get blessed. Ruth 4:13-17, ESV:

> [13] So Boaz took Ruth, and she became his wife. And he went in to her, and the Lord gave her conception, and she bore a son.

> [14] Then the women said to Naomi, "Blessed be the Lord, who has not left you this day without a redeemer, and may his name be renowned in Israel!

> [15] He shall be to you a restorer of life and a nourisher of your old age, for your daughter-in-law who loves you, who is more to you than seven sons, has given birth to him."

> [16] Then Naomi took the child and laid him on her lap and became his nurse.

> [17] And the women of the neighborhood gave him a name, saying, "A son has been born to Naomi." They named him Obed. He was the father of Jesse, the father of David.

God only wants to bless you. He does not want toxic emotions to destroy your soul.

Job 21:25, ESV:

> [25] Another dies in bitterness of soul, never having tasted of prosperity.

Ruminating about what you experience from another person hurting you drains your emotional energy and makes one fatigued.

A mature believer in the Lord knows it is wise to deal with hurt ASAP. As said earlier but it bears repeating think of ASAP standing for Always Say A Prayer.

Proverbs 14:10, NLT says:

10 Each heart knows its own bitterness, and no one else can fully share its joy.

Proverbs 15:13, NLT says:

13 A glad heart makes a happy face; a broken heart crushes the spirit.

Proverbs 16:24, NLT reads:

24 Kind words are like honey—sweet to the soul and healthy for the body.

God's Words are always sweet to our soul.

Proverbs 16:20, NLT says:

20 Those who listen to instruction will prosper; those who trust the Lord will be joyful.

The number 6 symbolizes man and human weakness, which is the evil of satan. The number 666 symbolizes the anti-Christ.

The Holy Spirit can help you to be strong if you just believe His ways are higher and wiser. In 2 Corinthians 12:7-10, ESV:

> 7 So to keep me from becoming conceited because of the surpassing greatness of the revelations, a thorn was given me in the flesh, a messenger of Satan to harass me, to keep me from becoming conceited.

> 8 Three times I pleaded with the Lord about this, that it should leave me.

> 9 But he said to me, "My grace is sufficient for you, for my power is made perfect in weakness." Therefore I will boast all the more gladly of my weaknesses, so that the power of Christ may rest upon me.

> 10 For the sake of Christ, then, I am content with weaknesses, insults, hardships, persecutions, and calamities. For when I am weak, then I am strong.

Bitterness can sometimes make a person feel helpless, which means intense misery from:

- Loss of a job
- Loss of a loved one
- Loss of freedom
- Losing your house
- Losing money in the 401K
- Losing limbs from your body
- Losing your car
- Losing your peace of mind
- Loss of hope
- Loss of health

Hezekiah cried bitterly for the loss of his health. In 2 Kings 20:1-7, ESV, it reads:

> 1 In those days Hezekiah became sick and was at the point of death. And Isaiah the prophet the son of Amoz came to him and said to him, "Thus says the Lord, 'Set your house in order, for you shall die; you shall not recover.'"

² Then Hezekiah turned his face to the wall and prayed to the Lord, saying,

³ "Now, O Lord, please remember how I have walked before you in faithfulness and with a whole heart, and have done what is good in your sight." And Hezekiah wept bitterly.

⁴ And before Isaiah had gone out of the middle court, the word of the Lord came to him:

⁵ "Turn back, and say to Hezekiah the leader of my people, Thus says the Lord, the God of David your father: I have heard your prayer; I have seen your tears. Behold, I will heal you. On the third day you shall go up to the house of the Lord,

⁶ and I will add fifteen years to your life. I will deliver you and this city out of the hand of the king of Assyria, and I will defend this city for my own sake and for my servant David's sake."

⁷ And Isaiah said, "Bring a cake of figs. And let them take and lay it on the boil, that he may recover."

Let me ask you a quick question. "What did Hezekiah do instantly when he heard bad news?"

The correct answer is prayed. The name Hezekiah means in the Hebrew "God gives strength."

When believers pray immediately, it prevents the mind from drifting and wandering into tormenting thoughts.

Isaiah 26:3, ESV reads:

³ You keep him in perfect peace whose mind is stayed on you, because he trusts in you.

Reread Chapter 1, "Put on the Attitude of Jesus." Jesus will keep all believers in perfect peace.

Bitterness does not have to turn into hate if you are angry at someone. A bitter heart cannot have true peace, but a forgiving heart always has true peaceful joy within. Studies have proven that negative emotions can damage the immune system and also your organs.

The Bible tells us to strive for peace in Hebrews 12:14-17, NLT:

> [14] Work at living in peace with everyone, and work at living a holy life, for those who are not holy will not see the Lord.
>
> [15] Look after each other so that none of you fails to receive the grace of God. Watch out that no poisonous root of bitterness grows up to trouble you, corrupting many.
>
> [16] Make sure that no one is immoral or godless like Esau, who traded his birthright as the firstborn son for a single meal.
>
> [17] You know that afterward, when he wanted his father's blessing, he was rejected.
>
> It was too late for repentance, even though he begged with bitter tears.

The more a believer gets rooted and digs deep into the Word of God, the more emotionally stable the person becomes and escapes the devil's traps. The Word of God in the Bible says in 2 Timothy 3:16, NLT,

> [16] All Scripture is inspired by God and is useful to teach us what is true and to make us realize what is wrong in our lives. It corrects us when we are wrong and teaches us to do what is right.

Godly thinking helps all believers to do what is right. We become emotionally free:

• When you allow God to examine your hearts. He gives you a new heart. The Bible tells us in Psalm 26:2-3 and Ezekiel 36:26, NIV:

> [2] Test me, Lord, and try me, examine my heart and my mind;
>
> [3] for I have always been mindful of your unfailing love and have lived in reliance on your faithfulness.
>
> [26] And I will give you a new heart, and I will put a new spirit

in you. I will take out your stony, stubborn heart and give you a tender, responsive heart.

By deciding to allow God to help you remove the toxic emotions to have a pure heart, you will be blessed. The Word of God explains the importance of this in 1 Peter 1:22, ESV, 1 John 3:3, NLT, and Matthew 5:8, NLT:

22 Having purified your souls by your obedience to the truth for a sincere brotherly love, love one another earnestly from a pure heart,

1 John 3:3

3 And all who have this eager expectation will keep themselves pure, just as he is pure.

Matthew 5:8

8 God blesses those whose hearts are pure, for they will see God.

• One must <u>believe</u> like King David that God can create a new heart within you.
Psalm 51:5-10, NLT:

5 For I was born a sinner—yes, from the moment my mother conceived me.
6 But you desire honesty from the womb, teaching me wisdom even there.
7 Purify me from my sins,[b] and I will be clean; wash me, and I will be whiter than snow.
8 Oh, give me back my joy again; you have broken me—now let me rejoice.
9 Don't keep looking at my sins. Remove the stain of my guilt.
10 Create in me a clean heart, O God. Renew a loyal spirit within me.

• One must <u>believe</u> God can strengthen you inwardly and heal your damaged heart only by His Spirit.

Ephesians 3:14-17, ESV reads:

> ¹⁴ For this reason I bow my knees before the Father,
>
> ¹⁵ from whom every family[a] in heaven and on earth is named,
>
> ¹⁶ that according to the riches of his glory he may grant you to be strengthened with power through his Spirit in your inner being,
>
> ¹⁷ so that Christ may dwell in your hearts through faith—that you, being rooted and grounded in love,

• By <u>asking</u> God to help you to forgive yourself and others, He will help you not to carry the emotional baggage around anymore. He can heal your crushed heart.

Matthew 7:7-8, ESV and Psalm 34:18, NIV:

> ⁷ "Ask, and it will be given to you; seek, and you will find; knock, and it will be opened to you.
>
> ⁸ For everyone who asks receives, and the one who seeks finds, and to the one who knocks it will be opened.

Psalm 34:18

> ¹⁸ The Lord is close to the brokenhearted and saves those who are crushed in spirit.

Having a true clean heart all believers can live out the abundant, blessed, and joyful life.
Hebrews 10:22, ESV says:

> ²² let us draw near with a true heart in full assurance of faith, with our hearts sprinkled clean from an evil conscience and our bodies washed with pure water.

John 10:10, NKJV reads:

[10] The thief does not come except to steal, and to kill, and to destroy. I have come that they may have life, and that they may have *it* more abundantly.

Matthew 5:1-12, NLT says:

[1] One day as he saw the crowds gathering, Jesus went up on the mountainside and sat down. His disciples gathered around him,

[2] and he began to teach them.

[3] "God blesses those who are poor and realize their need for him, for the Kingdom of Heaven is theirs.

[4] God blesses those who mourn, for they will be comforted.

[5] God blesses those who are humble, for they will inherit the whole earth.

[6] God blesses those who hunger and thirst for justice, for they will be satisfied.

[7] God blesses those who are merciful, for they will be shown mercy.

[8] God blesses those whose hearts are pure, for they will see God.

[9] God blesses those who work for peace, for they will be called the children of God.

[10] God blesses those who are persecuted for doing right, for the Kingdom of Heaven is theirs.

[11] "God blesses you when people mock you and persecute you and lie about you and say all sorts of evil things against you because you are my followers.

[12] Be happy about it! Be very glad! For a great reward awaits you in heaven. And remember, the ancient prophets were persecuted in the same way.

This is what God tells us about unbelievers in Titus 1:15, ESV: 15 To the pure, all things are pure, but to the defiled and unbelieving, nothing is pure; but both their minds and their consciences are defiled. Defiled means to make corrupt.

> ¹⁵ To the pure, all things are pure, but to the defiled and un-believing, nothing is pure; but both their minds and their consciences are defiled.

I pray all believers start to share their personal testimony to unbelievers to build God's Kingdom.
Holding grudges leads into a bitter attitude that makes a person more miserable, unhappy, and depressed. Luke 17:3-4, NLT tells us:

> ³ So watch yourselves! "If another believer sins, rebuke that person; then if there is repentance, forgive.
> ⁴ Even if that person wrongs you seven times a day and each time turns again and asks forgiveness, you must forgive."

The third toxic emotion Satan tries to get in our heart is **Fear**. Once again Isaiah 41:10, NLT, reads:

> ¹⁰ Don't be afraid, for I am with you. Don't be discouraged, for I am your God.
> I will strengthen you and help you. I will hold you up with my victorious right hand.

Zechariah 4:6, NLT explains:

> ⁶ Then he said to me, "This is what the Lord says to Zerub-babel: It is not by force nor by strength, but by my Spirit, says the Lord of Heaven's Armies.
> The spirit of fear is not the plan God has for his sons or daughters. Fear tries to paralyze you, but faith mobilizes you to stay focused and keep pressing on. You can run this Christian race successfully by depending and being humble on God's Supernatural strength and power. God has put His divine nature in you to liv a victorious life.

In 2 Timothy 1:7, NKJV, it states:

> ⁷ For God has not given us a spirit of fear, but of power and of love and of a sound mind.

Our Heavenly Father's unconditional love gave His Son Jesus godly power the night before the cross. Jesus was so humble and washed His disciples' feet. Jesus had a sound mind because He was under the control of the Holy Spirit.

There are two different kinds of fears, which are godly fear and ungodly fear. godly fear refers to a sense of respect and being obedient to His will and worshipping God only. Ungodly fear is being disrespectful and disobedient towards God's will. You can remember godly fear by using the word ROW.

R Respecting God
O Obeying God
W Worshipping God

God's will is for believers to have a healthy soul. The mind reflects what sinks into the heart. Now, a human heart that pumps blood through the body gives life. A lack of oxygen to the brain causes death, strokes, and memory loss. On the other hand, the emotional heart which is a conscious mental reaction.

The Holy Spirit makes a believer aware of the six toxic emotions which are anger, bitterness, fear, guilt, hate, and unforgiveness.

Remember the five gates the devil tries to enter into to destroy your soul and body. They are our mind, heart, eyes, ears and sex outside marriage. Fear does not belong in a believer's heart when they trust God. Proverbs 3:5-8, ESV, reads:

> [5]Trust in the Lord with all your heart, and do not lean on your own understanding.
>
> [6] In all your ways acknowledge him, and he will make straight your paths.
>
> [7] Be not wise in your own eyes; fear the Lord, and turn away from evil.
>
> [8] It will be healing to your flesh and refreshment[b] to your

bones.

God told Joshua not to fear the Egyptians in Deuteronomy 3:22, ESV:

> ²² You shall not fear them, for it is the Lord your God who fights for you.'

Moses told the people not to fear them also in Exodus 14:10-30, ESV:

> ¹⁰ When Pharaoh drew near, the people of Israel lifted up their eyes, and behold, the Egyptians were marching after them, and they feared greatly. And the people of Israel cried out to the Lord.
>
> ¹¹ They said to Moses, "Is it because there are no graves in Egypt that you have taken us away to die in the wilderness? What have you done to us in bringing us out of Egypt?
>
> ¹² Is not this what we said to you in Egypt: 'Leave us alone that we may serve the Egyptians'? For it would have been better for us to serve the Egyptians than to die in the wilderness."
>
> 13 And Moses said to the people, "Fear not, stand firm, and see the salvation of the Lord, which he will work for you today. For hthe Egyptians whom you see today, you shall never see again. 14 iThe Lord will fight for you, and you have only jto be silent."
>
> 15 The Lord said to Moses, "Why do you cry to me? Tell the people of Israel to go forward. 16 kLift up your staff, and stretch out your hand over the sea and divide it, that the people of Israel may go through the sea on dry ground. 17 And lI will harden the hearts of the Egyptians so that they shall go in after them, and mI will get glory over Pharaoh and all his host, his chariots, and his horsemen. 18 And the Egyptians nshall know that I am the Lord, mwhen I have gotten glory over Pharaoh, his chariots, and his horsemen."
>
> 19 oThen the angel of God who was going before the host of Israel moved and went behind them, and the pillar of cloud moved from before them and stood behind them, 20

coming between the host of Egypt and the host of Israel. And there was the cloud and the darkness. And it lit up the night1 without one coming near the other all night.

21 Then Moses stretched out his hand over the sea, and the Lord drove the sea back by pa strong east wind all night and made the sea dry land, and the waters were divided. 22 And the people of Israel went into the midst of the sea on dry ground, the waters being ta wall to them on their right hand and on their left. 23 The Egyptians pursued and went in after them into the midst of the sea, all Pharaoh's horses, his chariots, and his horsemen. 24 And in the morning watch the Lord in the pillar of fire and of cloud looked down on the Egyptian forces and threw the Egyptian forces into a panic, 25 clogging2 their chariot wheels so that they drove heavily. And the Egyptians said, "Let us flee from before Israel, for the uLord fights for them against the Egyptians." 26 Then the Lord said to Moses, "Stretch out your hand over the sea, that the water may come back upon the Egyptians, upon their chariots, and upon their horsemen." 27 wSo Moses stretched out his hand over the sea, and the sea returned to its normal course when the morning appeared. And as the Egyptians fled into it, the Lord ythrew3 the Egyptians into the midst of the sea. 28 The waters returned and covered the chariots and the horsemen; of all the host of Pharaoh that had followed them into the sea, anot one of them remained. 29 But the people of Israel walked on dry ground through the sea, the waters being a wall to them on their right hand and on their left. 30 Thus the Lord saved Israel that day from the hand of the Egyptians, and Israel saw the Egyptians dead on the seashore.

Yes, the Israelites were fearful and thought they were going to die in the wilderness until God divided the Red Sea. All of the Israelites walked through on dry ground. God will always rescue His people.

• God rescued the Jews from evil Haman and gave Esther favor to free the Jews.
• Our Heavenly Father let Daniel survive the lion's den. This story

is powerful.

Just because Daniel prayed within the 30 days when the King ordered everyone not to make a petition, Daniel was cast into the den of lions. Daniel 6:14-16, 19-27, ESV says:

> ¹⁴ Then the king, when he heard these words, was much distressed and set his mind to deliver Daniel. And he labored till the sun went down to rescue him.
>
> ¹⁵ Then these men came by agreement to the king and said to the king, "Know, O king, that it is a law of the Medes and Persians that no injunction or ordinance that the king establishes can be changed."
>
> ¹⁶ Then the king commanded, and Daniel was brought and cast into the den of lions. The king declared to Daniel, "May your God, whom you serve continually, deliver you!"
>
> ¹⁹ Then, at break of day, the king arose and went in haste to the den of lions.
>
> ²⁰ As he came near to the den where Daniel was, he cried out in a tone of anguish. The king declared to Daniel, "O Daniel, servant of the living God, has your God, whom you serve continually, been able to deliver you from the lions?"
>
> ²¹ Then Daniel said to the king, "O king, live forever!
>
> ²² My God sent his angel and shut the lions' mouths, and they have not harmed me, because I was found blameless before him; and also before you, O king, I have done no harm."
>
> ²³ Then the king was exceedingly glad, and commanded that Daniel be taken up out of the den. So Daniel was taken up out of the den, and no kind of harm was found on him, because he had trusted in his God.
>
> ²⁴ And the king commanded, and those men who had maliciously accused Daniel were brought and cast into the den of lions—they, their children, and their wives. And before they reached the bottom of the den, the lions overpowered them and broke all their bones in pieces.
>
> ²⁵ Then King Darius wrote to all the peoples, nations, and

languages that dwell in all the earth: "Peace be multiplied to you.

²⁶ I make a decree, that in all my royal dominion people are to tremble and fear before the God of Daniel, for he is the living God, enduring forever; his kingdom shall never be destroyed, and his dominion shall be to the end.

²⁷ He delivers and rescues; he works signs and wonders in heaven and on earth, he who has saved Daniel from the power of the lions."

Daniel was a praying man. Remember, a day without prayer is a day without godly power.

Now, David had Godly confidence when the enemies came against him.
Psalm 23:4, NLT says:

⁴ Even when I walk through the darkest valley, I will not be afraid, for you are close beside me. Your rod and your staff protect and comfort me.

Psalm 27:1-3, NLT reads:

¹ The Lord is my light and my salvation—so why should I be afraid? The Lord is my fortress, protecting me from danger, so why should I tremble?

² When evil people come to devour me, when my enemies and foes attack me, they will stumble and fall.

³ Though a mighty army surrounds me, my heart will not be afraid. Even if I am attacked, I will remain confident.

Psalm 34:4-10, NLT says:

⁴ I prayed to the Lord, and he answered me. He freed me from all my fears.

⁵ Those who look to him for help will be radiant with joy; no shadow of shame will darken their faces.

⁶ In my desperation I prayed, and the Lord listened; he saved

me from all my troubles.

⁷ For the angel of the Lord is a guard; he surrounds and defends all who fear him.

⁸ Taste and see that the Lord is good. Oh, the joys of those who take refuge in him!

⁹ Fear the Lord, you his godly people, for those who fear him will have all they need.

¹⁰ Even strong young lions sometimes go hungry, but those who trust in the Lord will lack no good thing.

1 Samuel 17:32-37, 40-51, NLT reads:

³² "Don't worry about this Philistine," David told Saul. "I'll go fight him!"

³³ "Don't be ridiculous!" Saul replied. "There's no way you can fight this Philistine and possibly win! You're only a boy, and he's been a man of war since his youth."

³⁴ But David persisted. "I have been taking care of my father's sheep and goats," he said. "When a lion or a bear comes to steal a lamb from the flock,

³⁵ I go after it with a club and rescue the lamb from its mouth. If the animal turns on me, I catch it by the jaw and club it to death.

³⁶ I have done this to both lions and bears, and I'll do it to this pagan Philistine, too, for he has defied the armies of the living God!

³⁷ The Lord who rescued me from the claws of the lion and the bear will rescue me from this Philistine!" Saul finally consented. "All right, go ahead," he said. "And may the Lord be with you!"

⁴⁰ He picked up five smooth stones from a stream and put them into his shepherd's bag. Then, armed only with his shepherd's staff and sling, he started across the valley to fight the Philistine.

⁴¹ Goliath walked out toward David with his shield bearer ahead of him,

⁴² sneering in contempt at this ruddy-faced boy.

⁴³ "Am I a dog," he roared at David, "that you come at me with a stick?" And he cursed David by the names of his gods.

⁴⁴ "Come over here, and I'll give your flesh to the birds and wild animals!" Goliath yelled.

⁴⁵ David replied to the Philistine, "You come to me with sword, spear, and javelin, but I come to you in the name of the Lord of Heaven's Armies—the God of the armies of Israel, whom you have defied.

⁴⁶ Today the Lord will conquer you, and I will kill you and cut off your head. And then I will give the dead bodies of your men to the birds and wild animals, and the whole world will know that there is a God in Israel!

⁴⁷ And everyone assembled here will know that the Lord rescues his people, but not with sword and spear. This is the Lord's battle, and he will give you to us!"

⁴⁸ As Goliath moved closer to attack, David quickly ran out to meet him.

⁴⁹ Reaching into his shepherd's bag and taking out a stone, he hurled it with his sling and hit the Philistine in the forehead. The stone sank in, and Goliath stumbled and fell face down on the ground.

⁵⁰ So David triumphed over the Philistine with only a sling and a stone, for he had no sword.

⁵¹ Then David ran over and pulled Goliath's sword from its sheath. David used it to kill him and cut off his head.

When the Philistines saw that their champion was dead, they turned and ran.

As strong Christian believers we can fight fear with God's Promises.

David had godly confidence that he could take Goliath down and kill him. As believers we can trust God to give us the victory. Jeremiah 29:11, NIV reads:

¹¹ For I know the plans I have for you," declares the Lord, "plans to prosper you and not to harm you, plans to give you hope and a future.

God wants to give all believers hope to cope.

Now let's read the story behind verse 11, in Jeremiah 29:4, Easy English Bible:

⁴ This is what the Lord All-Powerful, the God of the people of Israel, says to all the people he sent into captivity from Jerusalem to Babylon:

Why did God send the Israelites into captivity?

God sent the Israelites into captivity to discipline them for being rebellious, serving other gods, and being disobedient. They did not respect His authority. Jeremiah has been warning the Israelites of their corruption. Jeremiah 29:5-14, Easy English Bible:

⁵ "Build houses and live in them. Settle in the land. Plant gardens and eat the food you grow.

⁶ Get married and have sons and daughters. Find wives for your sons, and let your daughters be married. Do this so that they also may have sons and daughters. Have many children and grow in number in Babylon. Don't become fewer in number.

⁷ Also, do good things for the city I sent you to. Pray to the Lord for the city you are living in, because if there is peace in that city, you will have peace also."

⁸ The Lord All-Powerful, the God of the people of Israel, says, "Don't let your prophets and those who practice magic fool you. Don't listen to the dreams they have.

⁹ They are telling lies, and they are saying that their message is from me. But I didn't send it." This message is from the Lord.

¹⁰ This is what the Lord says: "Babylon will be powerful for 70 years. After that time, I will come to you people who are

living in Babylon. I will keep my good promise to bring you back to Jerusalem.

¹¹ I say this because I know the plans that I have for you." This message is from the Lord. "I have good plans for you. I don't plan to hurt you. I plan to give you hope and a good future.

¹² Then you will call my name. You will come to me and pray to me, and I will listen to you.

¹³ You will search for me, and when you search for me with all your heart, you will find me.

¹⁴ I will let you find me." This message is from the Lord. "And I will bring you back from your captivity. I forced you to leave this place. But I will gather you from all the nations and places where I have sent you," says the Lord, "and I will bring you back to this place."

God wants to bless His people but it is very essential for them to turn to him and repent of their disobedience. Judges 21:25, states in the NLT:

²⁵ In those days Israel had no king; all the people did whatever seemed right in their own eyes.

The Bible tells us God takes no pleasure in the death of wicked people in Ezekiel 33:10-20, NLT reads:

¹⁰ "Son of man, give the people of Israel this message: You are saying, 'Our sins are heavy upon us; we are wasting away! How can we survive?'

¹¹ As surely as I live, says the Sovereign Lord, I take no pleasure in the death of wicked people. I only want them to turn from their wicked ways so they can live. Turn! Turn from your wickedness, O people of Israel! Why should you die?

¹² "Son of man, give your people this message: The righteous behavior of righteous people will not save them if they turn to sin, nor will the wicked behavior of wicked people destroy them if they repent and turn from their sins.

¹³ When I tell righteous people that they will live, but then they sin, expecting their past righteousness to save them,

then none of their righteous acts will be remembered. I will destroy them for their sins.

¹⁴ And suppose I tell some wicked people that they will surely die, but then they turn from their sins and do what is just and right.

¹⁵ For instance, they might give back a debtor's security, return what they have stolen, and obey my life-giving laws, no longer doing what is evil. If they do this, then they will surely live and not die.

¹⁶ None of their past sins will be brought up again, for they have done what is just and right, and they will surely live.

¹⁷ "Your people are saying, 'The Lord isn't doing what's right,' but it is they who are not doing what's right.

¹⁸ For again I say, when righteous people turn away from their righteous behavior and turn to evil, they will die.

¹⁹ But if wicked people turn from their wickedness and do what is just and right, they will live.

²⁰ O people of Israel, you are saying, 'The Lord isn't doing what's right.' But I judge each of you according to your deeds."

Now, in Deuteronomy 28:1-14, NLT, it speaks on the blessings of obedience.

¹"If you fully obey the Lord your God and carefully keep all his commands that I am giving you today, the Lord your God will set you high above all the nations of the world.

² You will experience all these blessings if you obey the Lord your God:

³ Your towns and your fields will be blessed.

⁴ Your children and your crops will be blessed. The offspring of your herds and flocks will be blessed.

⁵ Your fruit baskets and breadboards will be blessed.

⁶ Wherever you go and whatever you do, you will be blessed.

⁷ "The Lord will conquer your enemies when they attack

you. They will attack you from one direction, but they will scatter from you in seven!

[8] "The Lord will guarantee a blessing on everything you do and will fill your storehouses with grain. The Lord your God will bless you in the land he is giving you.

[9] "If you obey the commands of the Lord your God and walk in his ways, the Lord will establish you as his holy people as he swore he would do.

[10] Then all the nations of the world will see that you are a people claimed by the Lord, and they will stand in awe of you.

[11] "The Lord will give you prosperity in the land he swore to your ancestors to give you, blessing you with many children, numerous livestock, and abundant crops.

[12] The Lord will send rain at the proper time from his rich treasury in the heavens and will bless all the work you do. You will lend to many nations, but you will never need to borrow from them.

[13] If you listen to these commands of the Lord your God that I am giving you today, and if you carefully obey them, the Lord will make you the head and not the tail, and you will always be on top and never at the bottom.

[14] You must not turn away from any of the commands I am giving you today, nor follow after other gods and worship them.

God only wants to bless His people and give them a sense of security. The Word of God tells us in Isaiah 32:18, NLT says:

[18] My people will live in safety, quietly at home. They will be at rest.

Let me share what God's love does for us in 1 John 4:13-21, NIV:

[13] This is how we know that we live in him and he in us: He has given us of his Spirit.

[14] And we have seen and testify that the Father has sent his

Son to be the Savior of the world.

¹⁵ If anyone acknowledges that Jesus is the Son of God, God lives in them and they in God.

¹⁶ And so we know and rely on the love God has for us. God is love. Whoever lives in love lives in God, and God in them.

¹⁷ This is how love is made complete among us so that we will have confidence on the day of judgment: In this world we are like Jesus.

¹⁸ There is no fear in love. But perfect love drives out fear, because fear has to do with punishment. The one who fears is not made perfect in love.

¹⁹ We love because he first loved us.

²⁰ Whoever claims to love God yet hates a brother or sister-is a liar. For whoever does not love their brother and sister, whom they have seen, cannot love God, whom they have not seen.

²¹ And he has given us this command: Anyone who loves God must also love their brother and sister.

God's love floods our soul with perfect peace because He gives us a sense of His Presence that fear does not grip our heart.

The old covenant led to condemnation, but the new covenant people's sins are forgiven and removed because Jesus paid the Sacrifice for our sin. In the old covenant an animal sacrifice only provided one year of covering people's sins. The blood of Jesus covers people's sins forever once we repent.

First John 1:9-10 and 1 John 2:1-3, NLT reads:

⁹ But if we confess our sins to him, he is faithful and just to forgive us our sins and to cleanse us from all wickedness.

¹⁰ If we claim we have not sinned, we are calling God a liar and showing that his word has no place in our hearts.

2 My dear children, I am writing this to you so that you will not sin. But if anyone does sin, we have an advocate who pleads our case before the Father. He is Jesus Christ, the one who is truly righteous.

2 He himself is the sacrifice that atones for our sins—and not only our sins but the sins of all the world.

3 And we can be sure that we know him if we obey his commandments.

By obeying God's commandments, believers are guilt free with no condemnation.

John 3:16-21, NLT, says:

16 "For this is how God loved the world: He gave[a] his one and only Son, so that everyone who believes in him will not perish but have eternal life.

17 God sent his Son into the world not to judge the world, but to save the world through him.

18 "There is no judgment against anyone who believes in him. But anyone who does not believe in him has already been judged for not believing in God's one and only Son.

19 And the judgment is based on this fact: God's light came into the world, but people loved the darkness more than the light, for their actions were evil.

20 All who do evil hate the light and refuse to go near it for fear their sins will be exposed.

21 But those who do what is right come to the light so others can see that they are doing what God wants."

Romans 8:1-6, NLT explains it very well, which says:

8 So now there is no condemnation for those who belong to Christ Jesus.

2 And because you belong to him, the power of the life-giving Spirit has freed you[b] from the power of sin that leads to death.

3 The law of Moses was unable to save us because of the weakness of our sinful nature. So God did what the law could not do. He sent his own Son in a body like the bodies we sinners have. And in that body God declared an end to sin's control over us by giving his Son as a sacrifice for our sins.

⁴ He did this so that the just requirement of the law would be fully satisfied for us, who no longer follow our sinful nature but instead follow the Spirit.

⁵ Those who are dominated by the sinful nature think about sinful things, but those who are controlled by the Holy Spirit think about things that please the Spirit.

⁶ So letting your sinful nature control your mind leads to death. But letting the Spirit control your mind leads to life and peace.

God can erase all your fears and give you hope. God knows the enemy uses fear to make one feel helpless and hopeless. Isaiah 43:1-3a, NIV:

> ¹But now, this is what the Lord says—he who created you, Jacob, he who formed you, Israel: "Do not fear, for I have redeemed you; I have summoned you by name; you are mine.

> ² When you pass through the waters, I will be with you; and when you pass through the rivers, they will not sweep over you. When you walk through the fire, you will not be burned; the flames will not set you ablaze.

> ³ For I am the Lord your God, the Holy One of Israel, your Savior;

Redeemed means to deliver from sin and its consequences by means of a sacrifice offered for the sinner.

Believers can have godly confidence like David. Psalm 23:4, NIV says:

> ⁴Even though I walk through the darkest valley, I will fear no evil, for you are with me; your rod and your staff, they comfort me. Fear not, God is with you. God can turn tragedy into victory.

The fourth toxic emotion is **Guilt**, and God does not want any believer to be weighted down with guilt.

1 John 1:9-10, 2:1-3, NLB:

⁹ But if we confess our sins to him, he is faithful and just to forgive us our sins and to cleanse us from all wickedness.

¹⁰ If we claim we have not sinned, we are calling God a liar and showing that his word has no place in our hearts.

2 My dear children, I am writing this to you so that you will not sin. But if anyone does sin, we have an advocate who pleads our case before the Father. He is Jesus Christ, the one who is truly righteous.

² He himself is the sacrifice that atones for our sins—and not only our sins but the sins of all the world.

³ And we can be sure that we know him if we obey his commandments.

The best words to say to someone or God are "forgive me," "I'm sorry," or "I apologize."

God is a merciful person, it tells us in Ephesians 2:1-5, NLT:

¹Once you were dead because of your disobedience and your many sins.
² You used to live in sin, just like the rest of the world, obeying the devil—the commander of the powers in the unseen world.[a] He is the spirit at work in the hearts of those who refuse to obey God.
³ All of us used to live that way, following the passionate desires and inclinations of our sinful nature. By our very nature we were subject to God's anger, just like everyone else.
⁴ But God is so rich in mercy, and he loved us so much,
⁵ that even though we were dead because of our sins, he gave us life when he raised Christ from the dead. (It is only by God's grace that you have been saved!)

Regardless of where your guilt is coming from, just know by not saying I'm sorry, forgive me, or I apologize, guilt can take root in your heart.

Proverbs 28:13, NLT says:

> 13 People who conceal their sins will not prosper, but if they confess and turn from them, they will receive mercy.

Satan wants to blind your eyes to God's love, mercy, and grace. God wants to open your eyes so you can be guilt-free.

In 2 Corinthians 4:4, and Psalm 146:8, NLT it reads:

> 4 Satan, who is the god of this world, has blinded the minds of those who don't believe. They are unable to see the glorious light of the Good News. They don't understand this message about the glory of Christ, who is the exact likeness of God.

Psalm 146:8

> 8 The Lord opens the eyes of the blind. The Lord lifts up those who are weighed down. The Lord loves the godly.

According to Dr. Mehmet Oz, guilt weakens your immune system, increases blood pressure, diabetes, depression, and anxiety.

Now, let me walk you through Romans on God's anger and judgment towards sin. Believers are dead to sin and a slave to righteousness.

Romans 1:18, 21-23, 28-32, NLT says:

> 18 But God shows his anger from heaven against all sinful, wicked people who suppress the truth by their wickedness.
>
> 21 Yes, they knew God, but they wouldn't worship him as God or even give him thanks. And they began to think up foolish ideas of what God was like. As a result, their minds became dark and confused.
>
> 22 Claiming to be wise, they instead became utter fools.
>
> 23 And instead of worshiping the glorious, ever-living God, they worshiped idols made to look like mere people and

birds and animals and reptiles.

28 Since they thought it foolish to acknowledge God, he abandoned them to their foolish thinking and let them do things that should never be done.

29 Their lives became full of every kind of wickedness, sin, greed, hate, envy, murder, quarreling, deception, malicious behavior, and gossip.

30 They are backstabbers, haters of God, insolent, proud, and boastful. They invent new ways of sinning, and they disobey their parents.

31 They refuse to understand, break their promises, are heartless, and have no mercy.

32 They know God's justice requires that those who do these things deserve to die, yet they do them anyway. Worse yet, they encourage others to do them, too.

Romans 2:4-8, 28-29, NLT says:

4 Don't you see how wonderfully kind, tolerant, and patient God is with you? Does this mean nothing to you? Can't you see that his kindness is intended to turn you from your sin?

5 But because you are stubborn and refuse to turn from your sin, you are storing up terrible punishment for yourself. For a day of anger is coming, when God's righteous judgment will be revealed.

6 He will judge everyone according to what they have done.

7 He will give eternal life to those who keep on doing good, seeking after the glory and honor and immortality that God offers.

8 But he will pour out his anger and wrath on those who live for themselves, who refuse to obey the truth and instead live lives of wickedness.

28 For you are not a true Jew just because you were born of Jewish parents or because you have gone through the ceremony of circumcision.

29 No, a true Jew is one whose heart is right with God. And true circumcision is not merely the letter of the law; rather, it is a change of heart produced by the Spirit. And a person with a changed heart seeks praise[a] from God, not from people.

Hebrews 10:22 in the NLT explains a change of heart:

22 let us go right into the presence of God with sincere hearts fully trusting him. For our guilty consciences have been sprinkled with Christ's blood to make us clean, and our bodies have been washed with pure water.

Jesus took our punishment; Romans 3:21-26 states:

21 But now God has shown us a way to be made right with him without keeping the requirements of the law, as was promised in the writings of Moses and the prophets long ago.

22 We are made right with God by placing our faith in Jesus Christ. And this is true for everyone who believes, no matter who we are.

23 For everyone has sinned; we all fall short of God's glorious standard.

24 Yet God, in his grace, freely makes us right in his sight. He did this through Christ Jesus when he freed us from the penalty for our sins.

25 For God presented Jesus as the sacrifice for sin. People are made right with God when they believe that Jesus sacrificed his life, shedding his blood. This sacrifice shows that God was being fair when he held back and did not punish those who sinned in times past,

26 for he was looking ahead and including them in what he would do in this present time. God did this to demonstrate his righteousness, for he himself is fair and just, and he makes sinners right in his sight when they believe in Jesus.

Do you believe you are the righteousness of God? Romans 4:20-25, NLT says:

²⁰ Abraham never wavered in believing God's promise. In fact, his faith grew stronger, and in this he brought glory to God.

²¹ He was fully convinced that God is able to do whatever he promises.

²² And because of Abraham's faith, God counted him as righteous.

²³ And when God counted him as righteous, it wasn't just for Abraham's benefit. It was recorded

²⁴ for our benefit, too, assuring us that God will also count us as righteous if we believe in him, the one who raised Jesus our Lord from the dead.

²⁵ He was handed over to die because of our sins, and he was raised to life to make us right with God.

The Bible tells us we are saved from God's judgment in Romans 5:9, NLT says:

⁹ And since we have been made right in God's sight by the blood of Christ, he will certainly save us from God's condemnation.

All believers who died with Jesus died to their sinful nature. Romans 6:1-11, NLT says:

¹Well then, should we keep on sinning so that God can show us more and more of his wonderful grace?

² Of course not! Since we have died to sin, how can we continue to live in it?

³ Or have you forgotten that when we were joined with Christ Jesus in baptism, we joined him in his death?

⁴ For we died and were buried with Christ by baptism. And just as Christ was raised from the dead by the glorious power of the Father, now we also may live new lives.

⁵ Since we have been united with him in his death, we will also be raised to life as he was.

⁶ We know that our old sinful selves were crucified with

Christ so that sin might lose its power in our lives. We are no longer slaves to sin.

7 For when we died with Christ we were set free from the power of sin.

8 And since we died with Christ, we know we will also live with him.

9 We are sure of this because Christ was raised from the dead, and he will never die again. Death no longer has any power over him.

10 When he died, he died once to break the power of sin. But now that he lives, he lives for the glory of God.

11 So you also should consider yourselves to be dead to the power of sin and alive to God through Christ Jesus.

Romans 6:18, 23, NLT says:

18 Now you are free from your slavery to sin, and you have become slaves to righteous living.

23 For the wages of sin is death, but the free gift of God is eternal life through Christ Jesus our Lord.

God is a very merciful God. He knows we are not perfect and makes mistakes. He will always forgive us because of the perfect sacrifice of Jesus dying on the cross for our sins.

Romans 8:1-6, NLT reads:

1 So now there is no condemnation for those who belong to Christ Jesus.

2 And because you belong to him, the power[a] of the life-giving Spirit has freed you from the power of sin that leads to death.

3 The law of Moses was unable to save us because of the weakness of our sinful nature So God did what the law could not do. He sent his own Son in a body like the bodies we sinners have. And in that body God declared an end to

sin's control over us by giving his Son as a sacrifice for our sins.

⁴ He did this so that the just requirement of the law would be fully satisfied for us, who no longer follow our sinful nature but instead follow the Spirit.

⁵ Those who are dominated by the sinful nature think about sinful things, but those who are controlled by the Holy Spirit think about things that please the Spirit.

⁶ So letting your sinful nature control your mind leads to death. But letting the Spirit control your mind leads to life and peace.

Read these scriptures about a clean consciences below. Hebrews 9:14, NIV:

¹⁴ How much more, then, will the blood of Christ, who through the eternal Spirit offered himself unblemished to God, cleanse our consciences from acts that lead to death so that we may serve the living God!

God is so merciful! Say these words out loud: I AM GUILT FREE!!

The fifth toxic emotion is **Hate**. Hating others is not from God. 1 John 3:10-18, NIV reads:

¹⁰ This is how we know who the children of God are and who the children of the devil are: Anyone who does not do what is right is not God's child, nor is anyone who does not love their brother and sister

¹¹ For this is the message you heard from the beginning: We should love one another.

¹² Do not be like Cain, who belonged to the evil one and murdered his brother. And why did he murder him? Because his own actions were evil and his brothers were righteous.

¹³ Do not be surprised, my brothers and sisters, if the world hates you.

¹⁴ We know that we have passed from death to life, because we love each other. Anyone who does not love remains in death.

¹⁵ Anyone who hates a brother or sister is a murderer, and you know that no murderer has eternal life residing in him.

¹⁶ This is how we know what love is: Jesus Christ laid down his life for us. And we ought to lay down our lives for our brothers and sisters.

¹⁷ If anyone has material possessions and sees a brother or sister in need but has no pity on them, how can the love of God be in that person?

¹⁸ Dear children, let us not love with words or speech but with actions and in truth.

An unloving nature is the devil's nature. Love reveals one's true nature.

1 John 4:7-12, NIV says:

⁷ Dear friends, let us love one another, for love comes from God. Everyone who loves has been born of God and knows God.
⁸ Whoever does not love does not know God, because God is love.
⁹ This is how God showed his love among us: He sent his one and only Son into the world that we might live through him.
¹⁰ This is love: not that we loved God, but that he loved us and sent his Son as an atoning sacrifice for our sins.
¹¹ Dear friends, since God so loved us, we also ought to love one another.
¹² No one has ever seen God; but if we love one another, God lives in us and his love is made complete in us.

A person who truly loves his brothers and sisters will not persecute or kill. Cain committed the first murder on earth. Do you know the reason why? Because Abel was a believer. Believers are to hate evil and overcome evil with good.

Romans 12:9-10, NIV, reads:

⁹ Love must be sincere. Hate what is evil; cling to what is good.

¹⁰ Be devoted to one another in love. Honor one another above yourselves.

Romans 12:17-21, NIV says:

¹⁷ Do not repay anyone evil for evil. Be careful to do what is right in the eyes of everyone.

¹⁸ If it is possible, as far as it depends on you, live at peace with everyone.

¹⁹ Do not take revenge, my dear friends, but leave room for God's wrath, for it is written: "It is mine to avenge; I will repay," says the Lord. ²⁰ On the contrary: "If your enemy is hungry, feed him; if he is thirsty, give him something to drink. In doing this, you will heap burning coals on his head."

²¹ Do not be overcome by evil, but overcome evil with good.

How do we know evil from good? We know people by their fruit. Is your fruit rotten or unrotten? Do you have a godly spirit or evil spirit? Do you have good fruit or bad fruit?

Galatians 5:22, NIV, says:

²² But the fruit of the Spirit is love, joy, peace, forbearance, kindness, goodness, faithfulness,

Unrotten Fruit

Love

Joy

Peace

Patience

Kindness

Goodness

Faithfulness

Gentleness

Self-Control

Rotten Fruit

Hate

Sadness

Chaos

Impatience

Meanness

Evil Doing

Unfaithfulness

Roughness

Lack of Self Control

Cain's jealousy turned into anger, bitterness and hate,, then to evil actions. God warned Cain about his out-of-control anger. Rockhead did kill Abel.

Genesis 4:3-7, NIV says:

> ³ In the course of time Cain brought some of the fruits of the soil as an offering to the Lord.
>
> ⁴ And Abel also brought an offering—fat portions from some of the firstborn of his flock. The Lord looked with favor on Abel and his offering,
>
> ⁵ but on Cain and his offering he did not look with favor. So, Cain was very angry, and his face was downcast.
>
> ⁶ Then the Lord said to Cain, "Why are you angry? Why is your face downcast?
>
> ⁷ If you do what is right, will you not be accepted? But if you do not do what is right, sin is crouching at your door; it desires to have you, but you must rule over it

Studies have proven that chronic emotional stress releases stress hormones such as adrenaline which increases heart rate and elevates blood pressure, cortisol increase sugars in the bloodstream, weakened immune system, and causes digestive problems. It also causes more anxiety, depression, weight gain, trouble concentrating, and difficult making wise decisions. Hate destroys our soul and body.

1 John 3:13-16, NIV

> ¹³ Do not be surprised, my brothers and sisters, if the world hates you.
>
> ¹⁴ We know that we have passed from death to life, because we love each other. Anyone who does not love remains in death.
>
> ¹⁵ Anyone who hates a brother or sister is a murderer, and you know that no murderer has eternal life residing in him.
>
> ¹⁶ This is how we know what love is: Jesus Christ laid down his life for us. And we ought to lay down our lives for our brothers and sisters. A person who truly loves will not:

- Hate others
- Hurt others
- Criticize others
- Abuse others
- Gossip about others
- Destroy others
- Murder others

Believers loves, cares, and want others to experience all the richness and blessing God offers

Philippians 2:4-5, NIV says:

4 not looking to your own interests but each of you to the interests of the others.

5 In your relationships with one another, have the same mindset as Christ Jesus:

Love is proof a believer passed from death to life but on the other hand if hate is in your heart, you remain in death. Let me restate 1 John 3:14, NIV:

14 We know that we have passed from death to life, because we love each other. Anyone who does not love remains in death.

Remains in death means to be spiritual dead. Here are some examples of spiritual death.

A person who wastes his life in wild living is spiritually dead. Luke 15:11-24, NLT reads

11 To illustrate the point further, Jesus told them this story: "A man had two sons. **12** The younger son told his father, 'I want my share of your estate now before you die.' So his father agreed to divide his wealth between his sons.

13 "A few days later this younger son packed all his belongings and moved to a distant land, and there he wasted all his money in wild living. **14** About the time his money ran out, a great famine swept over the land, and he began to starve. ¹⁵ He persuaded a local farmer to hire him, and the man sent him into his fields to feed the pigs. ¹⁶ The young man became so hungry that even the pods he was feeding the pigs looked good to him. But no one gave him anything.

¹⁷ "When he finally came to his senses, he said to himself, 'At home even the hired servants have food enough to spare, and here I am dying of hunger! ¹⁸ I will go home to my father and say, "Father, I have sinned against both heaven and you, ¹⁹ and I am no longer worthy of being called your son. Please take me on as a hired servant."'

²⁰ "So he returned home to his father. And while he was still a long way off, his father saw him coming. Filled with love and compassion, he ran to his son, embraced him, and kissed him. ²¹ His son said to him, 'Father, I have sinned against both heaven and you, and I am no longer worthy of being called your son.[a]'

²² "But his father said to the servants, 'Quick! Bring the finest robe in the house and put it on him. Get a ring for his finger and sandals for his feet. ²³ And kill the calf we have been fattening. We must celebrate with a feast, ²⁴ for this son of mine was dead and has now returned to life. He was lost, but now he is found.' So the party began.

A person who is separated from the life of God is said to be spiritually dead.

Ephesians 4:17-19, NLT tells us:

¹⁷ With the Lord's authority I say this: Live no longer as the Gentiles do, for they are hopelessly confused. ¹⁸ Their minds are full of darkness; they wander far from the life God gives because they have closed their minds and hardened their hearts against him. ¹⁹ They have no sense of shame. They live for lustful pleasure and eagerly practice every kind of impurity.

A person who does not have the Son of God is dead.

1 John 5:12, NIV says:

[12] Whoever has the Son has life; whoever does not have God's Son does not have life.

The meaning of spirit is the the nonphysical part of a person which is the seat of emotions and character.

The biblical definition of Spirit means to breathe, the wind, which is invisible, immaterial and powerful. Acts 2:1-4, NIV, John 3:5-8, NIV says:

[1] When the day of Pentecost came; they were all together in one place.

[2] Suddenly a sound like the blowing of a violent wind came from heaven and filled the whole house where they were sitting.

[3] They saw what seemed to be tongues of fire that separated and came to rest on each of them.

[4] All of them were filled with the Holy Spirit and began to speak in other tongues as the Spirit enabled them.

[5] Jesus answered, "Very truly I tell you, no one can enter the kingdom of God unless they are born of water and the Spirit.

[6] Flesh gives birth to flesh, but the Spirit[a] gives birth to spirit.

[7] You should not be surprised at my saying, 'You must be born again.'

[8] The wind blows wherever it pleases. You hear its sound, but you cannot tell where it comes from or where it is going. So it is with everyone born of the Spirit.

When a person has a spiritual mindset and right spiritual perspective, that person can manage life successfully in the supernatural Power of the Holy Spirit.

The last toxic emotion is on **Forgiveness**.

Matthew 6:14-15, NIV says:

¹⁴ For if you forgive other people when they sin against you, your heavenly Father will also forgive you.
¹⁵ But if you do not forgive others their sins, your Father will not forgive your sins.

Ephesians 4:26-27, 30-32, NIV says:

²⁶ "In your anger do not sin": Do not let the sun go down while you are still angry,
²⁷ and do not give the devil a foothold
³⁰ And do not grieve the Holy Spirit of God, with whom you were sealed for the day of redemption.
³¹ Get rid of all bitterness, rage and anger, brawling and slander, along with every form of malice.
³² Be kind and compassionate to one another, forgiving each other, just as in Christ God forgave you.

Hard feelings of anger, bitterness, fear, guilt, hate, is evidence that a person did not forgive the offender.

The word malice in verse 31, means the intention or desire to do evil. Evil people have a hostile impulse to inflict or injure another person. They do not think their wickedness is wrong. They think they have reason to do unkind, cruel, and heartless evil act. They stay unguilty until legal action are taken and justice is done. They do not have conscience and have no empathy for the human race.

A great illustration can be found in Matthew 18:21-35, NIV:

²¹ Then Peter came to Jesus and asked, "Lord, how many times shall I forgive my brother or sister who sins against me? Up to seven times?"
²² Jesus answered, "I tell you, not seven times, but seventy-seven times.
²³ "Therefore, the kingdom of heaven is like a king who wanted to settle accounts with his servants.
²⁴ As he began the settlement, a man who owed him ten

thousand bags of gold was brought to him.

²⁵ Since he was not able to pay, the master ordered that he and his wife and his children and all that he had be sold to repay the debt.

²⁶ "At this the servant fell on his knees before him. 'Be patient with me,' he begged, 'and I will pay back everything.'

²⁷ The servant's master took pity on him, canceled the debt and let him go.

²⁸ "But when that servant went out, he found one of his fellow servants who owed him a hundred silver coins. He grabbed him and began to choke him. 'Pay back what you owe me!' he demanded.

²⁹ "His fellow servant fell to his knees and begged him, 'Be patient with me, and I will pay it back.'

³⁰ "But he refused. Instead, he went off and had the man thrown into prison until he could pay the debt.

³¹ When the other servants saw what had happened, they were outraged and went and told their master everything that had happened.

³² "Then the master called the servant in. 'You wicked servant,' he said, 'I canceled all that debt of yours because you begged me to.

³³ Shouldn't you have had mercy on your fellow servant just as I had on you?'

³⁴ In anger his master handed him over to the jailers to be tortured, until he should pay back all he owed.

³⁵ "This is how my heavenly Father will treat each of you unless you forgive your brother or sister from your heart

The Bible tells us in Matthew 5:7, "Blessed are the merciful for they will be shown mercy".

The meaning of mercy is treating people with kindness and forgiveness, not cruel or harsh.

Unforgiveness poisons your soul and pollutes your body. When a person dwells on how a person hurt, abused, or did him or her wrong it causes the inability to think clearly. It also drains you emotionally, weakens immunity, causes high blood pressure, causes ulcers, heart attacks and strokes. This is all due to high levels of cortisol and adrenaline that comes when a person is emotional stressed out due to not forgiving one another.

Jesus and Stephen are the best examples for having a forgiving heart in the bible.

Jesus said these words when he was on the cross found in Luke 23:34, NIV:

> [34] Jesus said, "Father, forgive them, for they do not know what they are doing." And they divided up his clothes by casting lots.

Stephen said these words while he was being stoned to death. Acts 7:55-60, 8:1, NIV:

> [55] But Stephen, full of the Holy Spirit, looked up to heaven and saw the glory of God, and Jesus standing at the right hand of God.
> [56] "Look," he said, "I see heaven open and the Son of Man standing at the right hand of God."
> [57] At this they covered their ears and, yelling at the top of their voices, they all rushed at him,
> [58] dragged him out of the city and began to stone him. Meanwhile, the witnesses laid their coats at the feet of a young man named Saul.
> [59] While they were stoning him, Stephen prayed, "Lord Jesus, receive my spirit."
> [60] Then he fell on his knees and cried out, "Lord, do not hold this sin against them." When he had said this, he fell asleep.
> 8 And Saul approved of their killing him.

I'm sure you heard that 10% is what happens to us but 90% is how we respond.

Life is a series of choices and you get to decide when to let go of your hurt, anger, bitterness, fear, guilt, hate, so unforgiveness does not destroy your joy and peace of mind.

The devil cannot make believers mentally exhausted when we have the mind of Jesus.
Philippians 2:5, TLB

Your attitude should be the kind that was shown us by Jesus Christ,

The devil cannot drain us emotionally because we know the heart is so very deceitful.

Jeremiah 17:9-10, NIV says:
⁹ The heart is deceitful above all things and beyond cure.
Who can understand it?
¹⁰ "I the Lord search the heart and examine the mind, to reward each person according to their conduct, according to what their deeds deserve."

The devil cannot make us fatigued because God gives us sweet sleep.

Proverbs 3:24, ESV reads:
If you lie down, you will not be afraid; when you lie down, your sleep will be sweet.

²⁴The devil cannot destroy our soul when we believe we have Godly supernatural power to live life victoriously here on earth.

1 John 5:4-5, ESV says:
⁴ For everyone who has been born of God overcomes the world. And this is the victory that has overcome the world —our faith.
⁵ Who is it that overcomes the world except the one who

believes that Jesus is the Son of God

Romans 8:37, ESV reads:

[37] No, in all these things we are more than conquerors through him who loved us.

Say this prayer out loud if you need to forgive someone: "Heavenly Father, I am tired of being a victim. I believe you can heal all my hurts and pain. Help me to forgive (put the person's name in the blank). I believe you can restore my soul and give me victory and help me be an overcomer and help me forgive.

CHAPTER 4 SPIRITUAL EYES AND SPIRITUAL EARS WILL ENHANCE YOUR LIFE

Do you have good eyes or bad eyes?

Have your spiritual ears become dull?

The good heart is just like a good eye.

The eyes and ears are the entrance to the mind.

In Matthew 6:19-23, NIV, it states:

> [19] "Do not store up for yourselves treasures on earth, where moths and vermin destroy, and where thieves break in and steal.
>
> [20] But store up for yourselves treasures in heaven, where moths and vermin do not destroy, and where thieves do not break in and steal.
>
> [21] For where your treasure is, there your heart will be also.
>
> [22] "The eye is the lamp of the body. If your eyes are healthy, your whole body will be full of light.
>
> [23] But if your eyes are unhealthy, your whole body will be full of darkness. If then the light within you is darkness, how great is that darkness!

Being devoted to God keeps a believer's mind on heavenly riches. The Word of God tells us in Colossians 3:1-2, NIV:

Since, then, you have been raised with Christ, set your hearts on things above, where Christ is, seated at the right hand of God.

² Set your minds on things above, not on earthly things.

Earthly riches will decay and deteriorate. God does not want anyone to be consumed by material possessions. God wants us to be blessed, but not at the cost of being mentally stressed due to overspending. 2 Corinthians 4:18, NIV states:

¹⁸ So we fix our eyes not on what is seen, but on what is unseen, since what is seen is temporary, but what is unseen is eternal.

Proverbs 17:24, NLT says:

²⁴ Sensible people keep their eyes glued on wisdom, but a fool's eyes wander to the ends of the earth.

If a person's eyes are good and healthy, it grasps the true treasure in Heaven. Believers' hope is in heavenly riches. 1 Timothy 6:17, NIV says:

⁷ For we brought nothing into the world, and we can take nothing out of it.

Proverbs 10:22, NLT reads:

²² The blessing of the Lord makes a person rich, and he adds no sorrow with it.

He adds no sorrow means God makes believers comfortable and content in their riches. Paul speaks on how God wants all believers' eyes to be enlightened. In Ephesians 1:17-18, NIV, it says:

¹⁷ I keep asking that the God of our Lord Jesus Christ, the glorious Father, may give you the Spirit of wisdom and revelation, so that you may know him better.

¹⁸ I pray that the eyes of your heart may be enlightened in order that you may know the hope to which he has called you, the riches of his glorious inheritance in his holy people,

When a follower reads, listens, studies, and comprehends

God's promises, that is how the eyes of your heart are enlightened. The eyes are the window of your heart.

God wants all his sons and daughters to grow in knowledge. It is the Holy Spirit's responsibility to reveal to all who believe the deeper things of God. The Spirit of revelation is given when one seeks to know God more and more. Let these scriptures below penetrate your heart.

James 1:5-8, NIV reads:

> [5] If any of you lacks wisdom, you should ask God, who gives generously to all without finding fault, and it will be given to you.
>
> [6] But when you ask, you must believe and not doubt, because the one who doubts is like a wave of the sea, blown and tossed by the wind.
>
> [7] That person should not expect to receive anything from the Lord.
>
> [8] Such a person is double-minded and unstable in all they do.

None of us knows it all.

2 Corinthians 4:6, NIV says:

> [6] For God, who said, "Let light shine out of darkness," made his light shine in our hearts to give us the light of the knowledge of God's glory displayed in the face of Christ.

By letting the light of knowledge shine in your heart, you will gain clear understanding.

Psalms 119:130, NIV states:

> [130] The unfolding of your words gives light; it gives understanding to the simple.

If you are having a hard time understanding the Bible in the KJV, there are some other translations that are simple to comprehend:

- Easy English Bible
- New Living Translation
- English Revised Version
- English Standard Version

Hosea 4:6 and Job 36:7 in the NIV reads:

> [6] my people are destroyed from lack of knowledge. "Because you have rejected knowledge, I also reject you as my priests; because you have ignored the law of your God, I also will ignore your children.

> 7 He does not take his eyes off the righteous;
> he enthrones them with kings
> and exalts them forever.

Job 37:16 tells us of .."the wonders of him who hasperfect knowledge."

God does not want anyone to keep their eyes closed. He counsels us with His eyes. Isaiah 44:6-8, 18, ESV says:

> [6] Thus says the Lord, the King of Israel and his Redeemer, the Lord of hosts:
> "I am the first and I am the last; besides me there is no god.

> [7] Who is like me? Let him proclaim it. Let him declare and set it before me,
> since I appointed an ancient people. Let them declare what is to come, and what will happen.

> [8] Fear not, nor be afraid; have I not told you from of old and declared it?
> And you are my witnesses! Is there a God besides me? There is no Rock; I know not any."

> [18] They know not, nor do they discern, for he has shut their eyes, so that they cannot see, and their hearts, so that they cannot understand.

Psalms 32:8-9, ESV reads:

⁸ I will instruct you and teach you in the way you should go; I will counsel you with my eye upon you.

⁹ Be not like a horse or a mule, without understanding, which must be curbed with bit and bridle, or it will not stay near you.

God's eyes are on his sons and daughters. He does not want you to have a cast down eyes or haughty eyes. Psalms 42:11, ESV says:

¹¹ Why are you cast down, O my soul, and why are you in turmoil within me?
Hope in God; for I shall again praise him, my salvation and my God.

Remember the eyes are the windows to the heart. Are you discouraged or depressed? God can help you in your despair. Job 22:29 KJV says:

²⁹ When men are cast down, then thou shalt say, There is lifting up; and he shall save the humble person. It also speaks in Job 1:1, ESV that Job was a righteous man and had a pure heart:

1 There was a man in the land of Uz whose name was Job, and that man was blameless and upright, one who feared God and turned away from evil.

2 Corinthians 4:7-9, ESV states:

⁷ But we have this treasure in jars of clay, to show that the surpassing power belongs to God and not to us.

⁸ We are afflicted in every way, but not crushed; perplexed, but not driven to despair;

⁹ persecuted, but not forsaken; struck down, but not destroyed;

God is the author of order and not disorder. It says in 1 Corinthians 14:33, ESV:

³³ For God is not a God of confusion but of peace. As in all the churches of the saints,

The Holy Spirit helps believers to push the reset button and delete the downcast spirit which means low in spirit. We are the apple of his eyes. It tells us in Deuteronomy 32:10:

"He found him in a desert land, and in the howling waste of the wilderness; he encircled him, he cared for him, he kept him as the apple of his eye. Another set of eyes that God does not want believers to have is haughty eyes. Haughty means a person looking down on others and being arrogant with a prideful heart. Proverbs 6:16-19, NIV says:

[16] There are six things the Lord hates, seven that are detestable to him:

[17]   haughty eyes, a lying tongue, hands that shed innocent blood,

[18]   a heart that devises wicked schemes, feet that are quick to rush into evil,

[19]   a false witness who pours out lies and a person who stirs up conflict in the community.

God brings down a haughty spirit. It tells us in Psalms 18:27, NIV :

[27] You save the humble but bring low those whose eyes are haughty.

     God also opposes the proud. The Word of God speaks in James 4:6-7, NIV:

[6] But he gives us more grace. That is why Scripture says: "God opposes the proud
     but shows favor to the humble."

[7] Submit yourselves, then, to God. Resist the devil, and he will flee from you.

Humility is the state of being humble.

Proverbs 16:18, ESV says:

[18] Pride goes before destruction, and a haughty spirit before a fall.

Philippians 2:1-5, NIV, will sum this up:

2 Therefore if you have any encouragement from being

united with Christ, if any comfort from his love, if any common sharing in the Spirit, if any tenderness and compassion,

² then make my joy complete by being like-minded, having the same love, being one in spirit and of one mind.

³ Do nothing out of selfish ambition or vain conceit. Rather, in humility value others above yourselves,

⁴ not looking to your own interests but each of you to the interests of the others.

⁵ In your relationships with one another, have the same mindset as Christ Jesus: Matthew 13:10-17, NIV reads:

¹⁰ The disciples came to him and asked, "Why do you speak to the people in parables?"

¹¹ He replied, "Because the knowledge of the secrets of the kingdom of heaven has been given to you, but not to them.

¹² Whoever has will be given more, and they will have an abundance. Whoever does not have, even what they have will be taken from them.

¹³ This is why I speak to them in parables: "Though seeing, they do not see;

though hearing, they do not hear or understand.

¹⁴ In them is fulfilled the prophecy of Isaiah: "'You will be ever hearing but never understanding; you will be ever seeing but never perceiving.

¹⁵ For this people's heart has become calloused; they hardly hear with their ears,

and they have closed their eyes. Otherwise they might see with their eyes,

hear with their ears, understand with their hearts and turn, and I would heal them.'

¹⁶ But blessed are your eyes because they see, and your ears because they hear.

17 For truly I tell you, many prophets and righteous people longed to see what you see but did not see it, and to hear what you hear but did not hear it.

The reason why Jesus spoke in parables because Jesus knew he had an unbelieving crowd. The secrets were only given to believers. The unbelievers were blinded by satan and had deaf ears. 2 Corinthians 4:4 and Psalms 146:8 in the ESV tells us:

4 In their case the god of this world has blinded the minds of the unbelievers, to keep them from seeing the light of the gospel of the glory of Christ, who is the image of God.

8 the Lord opens the eyes of the blind. The Lord lifts up those who are bowed down; the Lord loves the righteous.

John 9:1-7, 18-23, 35-38, ESV explains Jesus heals a blind man's physical eyes but opens up his spiritual eyes and he becomes a believer:

9 As he passed by, he saw a man blind from birth. **2** And his disciples asked him, "Rabbi, who sinned, this man or his parents, that he was born blind?" **3** Jesus answered, "It was not that this man sinned, or his parents, but that the works of God might be displayed in him. **4** We must work the works of him who sent me while it is day; night is coming, when no one can work. **5** As long as I am in the world, I am the light of the world." **6** Having said these things, he spit on the ground and made mud with the saliva. Then he anointed the man's eyes with the mud **7** and said to him, "Go, wash in the pool of Siloam" (which means Sent). So he went and washed and came back seeing.**18** The Jews[a] did not believe that he had been blind and had received his sight, until they called the parents of the man who had received his sight **19** and asked them, "Is this your son, who you say was born blind? How then does he now see?" **20** His parents answered, "We know that this is our son and that he was born blind. **21** But how he now sees we do not know, nor do we know who opened his eyes. Ask him; he is of age. He will speak for himself." **22** (His parents said these things because they feared the Jews, for the Jews had already agreed that if anyone should confess Jesus[b] to be Christ, he was to be put out of the synagogue.) ²³ Therefore his parents said, "He is of age; ask him."³⁵ Jesus heard that they had cast him out, and having found him he said, "Do you believe in the Son of Man?"[a] ³⁶ He answered, "And who is he, sir, that I may believe in him?" ³⁷ Jesus said to him, "You have seen him, and it is he who is speaking to you." ³⁸ He said, "Lord, I believe," and he worshiped him.

Previously before Jesus healed the blind man, he tells the unbelievers in John 8:43-47, ESV:

> ⁴³ Why do you not understand what I say? It is because you cannot bear to hear my word.

> ⁴⁴ You are of your father the devil, and your will is to do your father's desires. He was a murderer from the beginning, and does not stand in the truth, because there is no truth in him. When he lies, he speaks out of his own character, for he is a liar and the father of lies.

> ⁴⁵ But because I tell the truth, you do not believe me.

> ⁴⁶ Which one of you convicts me of sin? If I tell the truth, why do you not believe me?

> ⁴⁷ Whoever is of God hears the words of God. The reason why you do not hear them is that you are not of God."

Believers are blessed with spiritual eyes and spiritual ears to have an abundant and blessed life. It speaks in John 20:24-31, ESV:

> ²⁴ Now Thomas, one of the twelve, called the Twin,[a] was not with them when Jesus came.

> ²⁵ So the other disciples told him, "We have seen the Lord." But he said to them, "Unless I see in his hands the mark of the nails, and place my finger into the mark of the nails, and place my hand into his side, I will never believe."

26 Eight days later, his disciples were inside again, and Thomas was with them. Although the doors were locked, Jesus came and stood among them and said, "Peace be with you."

27 Then he said to Thomas, "Put your finger here, and see my hands; and put out your hand, and place it in my side. Do not disbelieve, but believe."

28 Thomas answered him, "My Lord and my God!"

29 Jesus said to him, "Have you believed because you have seen me? Blessed are those who have not seen and yet have believed."

30 Now Jesus did many other signs in the presence of the disciples, which are not written in this book;

31 but these are written so that you may believe that Jesus is the Christ, the Son of God, and that by believing you may have life in his name.

Your spiritual eyes will be illuminated when you decide to not have deaf ears to God's promises. You may think, how do I get spiritual eyes? It can be found in Romans 10:17, ESV:

17 So faith comes from hearing, and hearing through the word of Christ.

The Bible tells us in John 10:27, ESV "my sheep hear my voice and I know them and they follow me".

When believers follow the Lord and use all five of their spiritual senses, they will hear the voice of God.

God wants us to listen to His word. Proverbs 2:1-10, ESV reads:

2 My son, if you receive my words and treasure up my commandments with you,

2 making your ear attentive to wisdom and inclining your heart to understanding;

3 yes, if you call out for insight and raise your voice for understanding,

⁴ if you seek it like silver and search for it as for hidden treasures,

⁵ then you will understand the fear of the Lord and find the knowledge of God.

⁶ For the Lord gives wisdom; from his mouth come knowledge and understanding;

⁷ he stores up sound wisdom for the upright; he is a shield to those who walk in integrity,

⁸ guarding the paths of justice and watching over the way of his saints.

⁹ Then you will understand righteousness and justice and equity, every good path;

¹⁰ for wisdom will come into your heart, and knowledge will be pleasant to your soul;

By reading and seeing God's word, he speaks to your heart. 2 Timothy 2:15, KJV says:

¹⁵ Study to shew thyself approved unto God, a workman that needeth not to be ashamed, rightly dividing the word of truth.

To taste the Word involves sampling. To see involves understanding. Chewing and digesting the Word you will experience God's goodness. Psalms 34:8, ESV says:

⁸ Oh, taste and see that the Lord is good! Blessed is the man who takes refuge in him!

Taking refuge in Jesus means we have a sense of security, sense of safety by trusting and staying in God's presence. As believers, we are called sheep and the shepherd knows how to take care of his sheep. As we chew on the word of God's promises like sheep physical digest system, we can spiritually digest the word of God easier. Sheep rechew and re-swallow their food after regurgitating.

Believers who do not chew spiritual food well develop digestive problems and become spiritual malnourished. The word of God will never penetrate their heart. One must keep their taste buds sweet with God's Word.

The Holy Spirit wants to touch your heart with the words in the Bible. One touch from Jesus can heal you mentally, emotionally, and physically. Matthew 8:1-3 in the NLT speaks on the touch of Jesus. Jesus has healing supernatural power. All of the believers wanted to touch Jesus. It tells us in Luke 6:17-19, NLT:

> [17] When they came down from the mountain, the disciples stood with Jesus on a large, level area, surrounded by many of his followers and by the crowds. There were people from all over Judea and from Jerusalem and from as far north as the seacoasts of Tyre and Sidon.

> [18] They had come to hear him and to be healed of their diseases; and those troubled by evil spirits were healed.

> [19] Everyone tried to touch him, because healing power went out from him, and he healed everyone.

Another great healing story was a woman of faith who believed that if she just touched the hem of Jesus' garment, she would be healed. The story is found in Mark 5:25-34, NLT.

God does not just heal the body, but the mind and heart which is your soul. Psalms 34:17-18, ESV reads:

> [17] When the righteous cry for help, the Lord hears and delivers them out of all their troubles.

> [18] The Lord is near to the brokenhearted and saves the crushed in spirit.

God can heal your wounded heart that comes from trouble, painful, and hurtful thoughts. Psalms 147:3, in the ESV and Matthew 5:4 in the NLT tells us about our true comforter.

> [3] He heals the brokenhearted and binds up their wounds.

> [4] God blesses those who mourn, for they will be comforted.

As believers hear the Word of God from others, read and see the scriptures in the Bible and taste and digest the Word of God, they will experience God's touch that heal their soul and body.

All believers are responsible to let unbelievers smell the

sweet aroma from the Holy Spirit presence. Others need to know the words in the Bible are sweet smelling words of expensive perfume.

2 Corinthians 2:14-16, NLT explains it well which says:

> [14] But thank God! He has made us his captives and continues to lead us along in Christ's triumphal procession. Now he uses us to spread the knowledge of Christ everywhere, like a sweet perfume.
>
> [15] Our lives are a Christ-like fragrance rising up to God. But this fragrance is perceived differently by those who are being saved and by those who are perishing.
>
> [16] To those who are perishing, we are a dreadful smell of death and doom. But to those who are being saved, we are a life-giving perfume. And who is adequate for such a task as this?

God wants to hear your prayer. 1 Peter 3:8-12 tells us in the NLT:

> [8] Finally, all of you should be of one mind. Sympathize with each other. Love each other as brothers and sisters. Be tenderhearted, and keep a humble attitude.
>
> [9] Don't repay evil for evil. Don't retaliate with insults when people insult you. Instead, pay them back with a blessing. That is what God has called you to do, and he will grant you his blessing.
>
> [10] For the Scriptures say, "If you want to enjoy life and see many happy days,
> keep your tongue from speaking evil and your lips from telling lies.
>
> [11] Turn away from evil and do good. Search for peace, and work to maintain it.
>
> [12] The eyes of the Lord watch over those who do right, and his ears are open to their prayers. But the Lord turns his face against those who do evil.

CHAPTER 5 STRESS MANAGEMENT GOD'S WAY

Get a piece of paper ready and pen. Are you ready to take a stress test to see your level of stress?

Psalms 18:6, ESV reads:

> [6] In my distress I called upon the Lord; to my God I cried for help.
> From his temple he heard my voice, and my cry to him reached his ears.

Are you crying out to God in prayer? The Bible has all the answers to help believers to manage stress successfully. One must be aware of their stress level to make positive changes to enhance their life and be able to relax, mellow out, chill out, or unwind. What level are you?

Let's take the stress test together. There are no right or wrong answers.

- 1 Means Never
- 2 Means Sometimes
- 3 Means Frequently
- 4 Means Always

I try to do as much as possible in the least amount of time.

I become impatient with delays or interruptions and other employees who seem to be working to slowly.

I always have to win at games to enjoy myself.

I speed up the car to get through amber lights.

I am unlikely to ask for or indicate I need help with a problem for fear of appearing weak.

I constantly seek the respect and admiration of others.

I am overly critical of the way others do their work.

I have the habit of looking at my watch or the clock often.

I constantly strive to better my position and achievement.

I tend to spread myself "too-thin" in terms of time.

I have the habit of doing more than one thing at a time.

I frequently get angry or irritable.

I have little time for hobbies or time by myself.

I have the tendency to talk quickly or hasten conversations.

I consider myself "hard-driving".

My friends and/or relative consider me hard-driving.

I have the tendency to get involved in multiple projects, and while I'm involved in one activity, I'm thinking of other things that need to be done at the same time.

I feel vaguely guilty if I relax and do nothing during my free moments.

I take on too many responsibilities.

I drink or take drugs to calm my nerves.

I am afraid of being passed over by my company or having no control over the company's future.

I suffer from ulcers or a nervous stomach.

I am a workaholic – tending to work 60-70 hour weeks instead of the normal 40 hour week.

Now that you are aware of your stress levels, let's see where your number level means:

20-30 – chances are you are non-productive or your job lacks stimulation.

30-50 – you have a good balance between stress and controlling it.

50-60 – you are marginally too tense; you aren't handling stress too well.

60-80 – your health may be at risk due to your high stress level.

A high stress level for a long time can lead into serious health problems due to stress hormones getting released

Some of the physical signs are:

- Headache
- Difficulty concentrating
- Fatigue
- Upset stomach
- Insomnia

The serious physical signs are:

- High blood pressure
- Abnormal heartbeat
- Hardening of the arteries
- Heart disease
- Heart attacks
- Heartburn
- Irritable bowel syndrome
- Constipation or diarrhea
- Depression
- Weight gain or loss
- Flare up of asthma or arthritis

According to WebMD.com

3 John 1:2, NKJV reads:

> 2 Beloved, I pray that you may prosper in all things and be in health, just as your soul prospers

God healed me from anxiety attacks 30 years ago. By becoming aware of what causes your stress you can reduce your stress level to cope and have better coping strategies.

2 Corinthians 4:7-10 in the NKJV reads:

7 But we have this treasure in earthen vessels, that the excellence of the power may be of God and not of us. 8 We are hard-pressed on every side, yet not crushed; we are perplexed, but not in despair; 9 persecuted, but not forsaken; struck down, but not destroyed— 10 always carrying about in the body the dying of the Lord Jesus, that the life of Jesus also may be manifested in

our body.

Here are some meanings in verses 8 and 9 so you can get the full message in your spirit

Hard pressed – to be oppressed, pressured or troubled.

Crushed – to be kept in a cramped place or be distressed.

Perplexed – to be at a loss wondering which way to go and unable to find an answer.

Despair – to be hopeless to have no confidence or assurance, to be without any sense of security.

God's supernatural divine power brings us out from despair to victory. He gives us hope and godly confidence to endure. The Bible says it in Romans 15:4-5 in the NIV.

> [4] For everything that was written in the past was written to teach us, so that through the endurance taught in the Scriptures and the encouragement they provide we might have hope.
>
> [5] May the God who gives endurance and encouragement give you the same attitude of mind toward each other that Christ Jesus had, While I have these next verses already on the previous page, I will show it in another translation for more insight.

1 Corinthians 4:7-10 in the NIV reads: 7 But we have this treasure in jars of clay to show that this all-surpassing power is from God and not from us. 8 We are hard pressed on every side, but not crushed; perplexed, but not in despair; 9 persecuted, but not abandoned; struck down, but not destroyed. 10 We always carry around in our body the death of Jesus, so that the life of Jesus may also be revealed in our body.

Here are some other meanings of the words in this scripture.

Persecuted – to treat someone unfairly over a long period of time because of their race, religion or political beliefs.

Abandoned – left without needed protection, care or support.

Struck down – to be knocked down to make an attack on or to kill.

Destroyed – to ruin someone mentally, emotionally and physically

John 10:10, NJKV reads:

> ^{10} The thief does not come except to steal, and to kill, and to destroy. I have come that they may have life, and that they may have *it* more abundantly.

The Holy Spirit's presence will sustain all believers with godly power within. Ephesians 3:16-20 in the NIV reads:

> ^{16} I pray that out of his glorious riches he may strengthen you with power through his Spirit in your inner being,
>
> ^{17} so that Christ may dwell in your hearts through faith. And I pray that you, being rooted and established in love,
>
> ^{18} may have power, together with all the Lord's holy people, to grasp how wide and long and high and deep is the love of Christ,
>
> ^{19} and to know this love that surpasses knowledge—that you may be filled to the measure of all the fullness of God.
>
> ^{20} Now to him who is able to do immeasurably more than all we ask or imagine, according to his power that is at work within us,

God empowers believers to get through the top five stressors which are death of a loved one or close friend, divorce, moving, health issues, and loss of a job.

Now I hope you have godly confidence knowing and believing God cares so deeply about your heart issues. The Bible has spiritual coping skills to deal with life problems here on earth. Here are some coping mechanisms to release emotional stress.

Breathing deeply slows down the heartbeat and lowers blood pressure. The breath of God gives us life and not anxiety attacks.

Genesis 2:7, NIV says:

> [7] Then the Lord God formed a man[a] from the dust of the ground and breathed into his nostrils the breath of life, and the man became a living being.

Praying scriptures to our heavenly Father and asking in Jesus' name will minimize the effects of stress to our bodies. Prayer increases godly confidence and bring peace of mind. Prayer promotes humility, improves attitude, and relieves stress. Phillipians 4:6-9, NLT says:

> [6] Do not be anxious about anything, but in every situation, by prayer and petition, with thanksgiving, present your requests to God.
>
> [7] And the peace of God, which transcends all understanding, will guard your hearts and your minds in Christ Jesus.
>
> [8] Finally, brothers and sisters, whatever is true, whatever is noble, whatever is right, whatever is pure, whatever is lovely, whatever is admirable—if anything is excellent or praiseworthy—think about such things.
>
> [9] Whatever you have learned or received or heard from me, or seen in me—put it into practice. And the God of peace will be with you.

Walking in the Spirit is extremely beneficial when we die to our ugly sinful flesh. The Holy Spirit helps us to walk in peace. Galations 5:16-17 in the NIV reads:

> [16] So I say, walk by the Spirit, and you will not gratify the desires of the flesh.
>
> [17] For the flesh desires what is contrary to the Spirit, and the Spirit what is contrary to the flesh. They are in conflict with each other, so that you are not to do whatever[a] you want.

Talking to someone you trust takes the lid off the pressure cooker to alleviate built up emotional steam.

Proverbs 15:22, in the NIV reads:

> ²² Plans fail for lack of counsel, but with many advisers they succeed.

Journaling is an emotional release and helps get rid of negative thoughts. It inspires us to think of possible solutions. It gives us crystal clear thinking. Deuteronomy 6:5-9 in the NIV reads:

> ⁵ Love the Lord your God with all your heart and with all your soul and with all your strength.

> ⁶ These commandments that I give you today are to be on your hearts.

> ⁷ Impress them on your children. Talk about them when you sit at home and when you walk along the road, when you lie down and when you get up.

> ⁸ Tie them as symbols on your hands and bind them on your foreheads.

> ⁹ Write them on the doorframes of your houses and on your gates.

Writing scriptures down that pertain to our problems reduce pressure.

Crying is not a sign of weakness. Shedding emotional tears releases endorphins and improves our mood. It calms our nervous system down and promotes a sense of well being.

Psalms 30:5 in the NKJV reads:

> ⁵ ...Weeping may endure for a night, But joy *comes* in the morning.

Exercising stimulates part of our brain and releases natural hormones which as endorphins, dopamine (do pa meon), serotonin (seer ru tow in), and norephinephrine (naw rep puh neph in), which lowers stress hormones that damage our bodies. These happy natural hormones give us the runner's high and help relieve stress, pain and depression. 1 Timothy 4:7-10 in the NLT reads:

⁷ Do not waste time arguing over godless ideas and old wives' tales. Instead, train yourself to be godly.

⁸ "Physical training is good, but training for godliness is much better, promising benefits in this life and in the life to come."

⁹ This is a trustworthy saying, and everyone should accept it.

¹⁰ This is why we work hard and continue to struggle,[a] for our hope is in the living God, who is the Savior of all people and particularly of all believers.

Laughing enhances our intake on oxygen and stimulates our lungs, heart, and muscles. It also increases the happy hormone called endorphins that gets released from our brain. It is a great way to deal with anxiety.

Proverbs 17:22 tells us in NLT:

²² A cheerful heart is good medicine, but a broken spirit saps a person's strength.

Eating healthy increases serotonin which calms the soul and cuts down on cortisol and adrenaline stress hormones that harm our bodies.

Proverbs 25:16 in NLT speaks about too much honey will make you sick. God wants us to have a balanced diet.

Sleeping is very well needed. A good night sleep gives us energy and we are more alert. Proper sleep increases serotonin and helps prevent deep depression.

Proverbs 3:24 in the ESV reads:

²⁴ If you lie down, you will not be afraid; when you lie down, your sleep will be sweet.

I hope you pick one or two of these coping mechanisms and you never quit. Jesus cares deeply for all of us and loves us all unconditionally. Jesus can deliver your troubled heart.

The Bible says in John 14:1-3, in the NIV:

"Do not let your hearts be troubled. You believe in God; believe also in me.

² My Father's house has many rooms; if that were not so, would I have told you that I am going there to prepare a place for you?

³ And if I go and prepare a place for you, I will come back and take you to be with me that you also may be where I am.

Jesus was talking to his followers because they were deeply troubled. Things happened that disturbed their soul. Jesus told his disciples he was leaving this earth. The words Jesus says is found in John 13:33 in the NIV, which reads: "My children, I will be with you only a little longer. You will look for me, and just as I told the Jews, so I tell you now: Where I am going, you cannot come.

Deliverance from a troubled heart comes through trusting in God's son Jesus and believing Jesus is the Son of God. These four scriptures will explain: Psalm 107:6, ESV: Then they cried to the Lord in their trouble, and he delivered them from their distress.

John 20:31, NIV reads:

³¹ But these are written that you may believe[a] that Jesus is the Messiah, the Son of God, and that by believing you may have life in his name.

John 5:24, NIV reads:

²⁴ "Very truly I tell you, whoever hears my word and believes him who sent me has eternal life and will not be judged but has crossed over from death to life.

John 3:36, NIV says:

³⁶ Whoever believes in the Son has eternal life, but whoever rejects the Son will not see life, for God's wrath remains on them.

Deliverance means to cleanse people of demons and evil

spirits. To sum it all up, whoever rejects the Son of Jesus will not have eternal life and will be condemned. John 3:16-20, tells us in the NKJV:

> **16** For God so loved the world that He gave His only begotten Son, that whoever believes in Him should not perish but have everlasting life.
>
> **17** For God did not send His Son into the world to condemn the world, but that the world through Him might be saved.
>
> **18** "He who believes in Him is not condemned; but he who does not believe is condemned already, because he has not believed in the name of the only begotten Son of God.
>
> **19** And this is the condemnation, that the light has come into the world, and men loved darkness rather than light, because their deeds were evil.
>
> **20** For everyone practicing evil hates the light and does not come to the light, lest his deeds should be exposed.

Philippians 4:6-7, Amplified Bible says:

> **6** Do not be anxious *or* worried about anything, but in everything [every circumstance and situation] by prayer and petition with thanksgiving, continue to make your [specific] requests known to God.
>
> **7** And the peace of God [that peace which reassures the heart, that peace] which transcends all understanding, [that peace which] stands guard over your hearts and your minds in Christ Jesus [is yours].

The word garrison means a body of troops stationed in a particular location, to guard it. It is a perfect superintendent.

Another word for superintendent is overseer. God has anointed ministers to teach believers to guard their soul which is a believer's mind and emotions. 1 Timothy 3:1, NIV reads:

> Here is a trustworthy saying: Whoever aspires to be an overseer desires a noble task.

A noble task is one who is dedicated to help others to

become spiritually mature to manage stress successfully.

Ephesians 4:11-13, NIV says:

[11] So Christ himself gave the apostles, the prophets, the evangelists, the pastors and teachers,

[12] to equip his people for works of service, so that the body of Christ may be built up

[13] until we all reach unity in the faith and in the knowledge of the Son of God and become mature, attaining to the whole measure of the fullness of Christ. Believers become mature by applying Hebrews 13:7, and 17, NIV which reads:

[7] Remember your leaders, who spoke the word of God to you.

[17] Have confidence in your leaders and submit to their authority, because they keep watch over you as those who must give an account. Do this so that their work will be a joy, not a burden, for that would be of no benefit to you.

Jesus was under unbearable stress, but he knew in order to have the victory, he needed to pray. He endured the cross and maintained a clear sense of His Father's purpose. Mark 14:32-36, NIV reads:

[32] They went to a place called Gethsemane, and Jesus said to his disciples, "Sit here while I pray."

[33] He took Peter, James and John along with him, and he began to be deeply distressed and troubled.

[34] "My soul is overwhelmed with sorrow to the point of death," he said to them. "Stay here and keep watch."

[35] Going a little farther, he fell to the ground and prayed that if possible the hour might pass from him.

[36] "Abba,[a] Father," he said, "everything is possible for you. Take this cup from me. Yet not what I will, but what you will."

Moses was overwhelmed with stress trying to keep over two million Israelites happy as they wandered in the wilderness. God lightened his stress load. Numbers 11:14-17, NIV reads:

> [14] I cannot carry all these people by myself; the burden is too heavy for me.
>
> [15] If this is how you are going to treat me, please go ahead and kill me—if I have found favor in your eyes—and do not let me face my own ruin."
>
> [16] The Lord said to Moses: "Bring me seventy of Israel's elders who are known to you as leaders and officials among the people. Have them come to the tent of meeting, that they may stand there with you.
>
> [17] I will come down and speak with you there, and I will take some of the power of the Spirit that is on you and put it on them. They will share the burden of the people with you so that you will not have to carry it alone.

God has the knowledge and wisdom in the Bible to lighten all believer's stress load.

Matthew 11:28-30, NIV reads:

> [28] "Come to me, all you who are weary and burdened, and I will give you rest.
>
> [29] Take my yoke upon you and learn from me, for I am gentle and humble in heart, and you will find rest for your souls.
>
> [30] For my yoke is easy and my burden is light."

Let me reread Philippians 4:6-7, NIV and explain how prayer is the main key to the answer to worrying, fear, or anxiety.

Prayers refers to making our request known to God and asking in Jesus' name. Believes must make time to listen to God to get the best benefits. Consistent prayer energizes believers as they expect the best outcome in their situation.

A day without prayer is a day without godly power.

Once again, think of ASAP which normally stands for as soon

as possible. As I have stated before it bears repeating that ASAP can stand for Always Say A Prayer. Ephesians 6:18, NLT reads:

¹⁸ Pray in the Spirit at all times and on every occasion. Stay alert and be persistent in your prayers for all believers everywhere

The word <u>petition</u> in this scripture refers to pouring out our soul to God with a humble request as we pray about a special need.

God is interested in all the details of our life. God wants all believers to cry out to Him in prayer. Psalms 102:1, NLT says: Lord, hear my prayer! Listen to my plea!

The word <u>thanksgiving</u> means while we pray, we always give God the praise for all he carries us through and has done for us. Psalms 106:1, NLT says:

¹ Praise the Lord! Give thanks to the Lord, for he is good! His faithful love endures forever.

Psalms 107:21-22, NLT tells us:

²¹ Let them praise the Lord for his great love and for the wonderful things he has done for them.

²² Let them offer sacrifices of thanksgiving and sing joyfully about his glorious acts.

The word <u>request</u> means as we pray, be very specific with our words and tell God in detail our request and ask in Jesus' name. John 14:13-14, ESV reads:

¹³ Whatever you ask in my name, this I will do, that the Father may be glorified in the Son.

¹⁴ If you ask me[a] anything in my name, I will do it.

Matthew 7:7, ESV tells us:

⁷ "Ask, and it will be given to you; seek, and you will find; knock, and it will be opened to you. Keep asking, keep seeking, keep knocking!

1 Peter 5:7, ESV says:

[7] casting all your anxieties on him, because he cares for you. Jesus loves us unconditionally.

Don't Let anything steal your peace of mind! Love you all brothers and sisters. Stay connected with me on Facebook under my name or under Teaching God's Promises.

Connect with Yvonne Tiburzi Knotts
On Facebook under "Teaching God's Promises"

Made in the USA
Middletown, DE
12 July 2022